WARBONNETS

WARBONNETS

From *to*
Super Chief *Super Fleet*

Dan Pope and Mark Lynn

FRONT JACKET PHOTO:

A pair of Warbonnet PA-1s leads an excursion train through Victorville (Calif.) Narrows in February 1964. The three-car special, sponsored by Orange Empire Trolley Museum, made a Los Angeles-Barstow round trip over Cajon Pass. **Jim Walker**

REAR JACKET PHOTO:

Flanges squeal in protest against the sharp curvature as Dash 8-40BW 517 and three more units struggle up California's Tehachapi Pass with the second section of the 971 train, an expedited Richmond-Chicago run heavy with refrigerated trailers loaded with produce from the farmlands of the Central Valley. **Bryan G. Moseley**

FRONT AND REAR ENDPAPERS:

Chard Walker, one of the pioneer photographers of Cajon Pass, offers a look at the eastbound *Grand Canyon* working upgrade through Sullivan's Curve. A five-unit set of F3s lugs a 21-car train toward the Summit—and Chard's home—on July 4, 1964. Chard was a Santa Fe operator at the Summit station and had a house two doors down from the depot. **Chard Walker**

TITLE PAGE:

The Indian headdress emblem worn on the side of early Warbonnet locomotives. **K.B. King Jr**.

FRONTICEPIECE:

A new generation of Warbonnets is represented by a quartet of Dash 8-40BWs leading an eastbound Maersk stack train as it climbs Goffs Hill in California's Mojave Desert in January 1991. **Brian Solomon**

Edited by Don Gulbrandsen
and Paul Hammond

Dust jacket design by Alan Barrett

Book design and layout by Katie Danneman

Published by Pentrex, Inc.
P.O. Box 94911
Pasadena, California 91109

Manufactured in the United States of America.

ISBN 1-56342-004-X

♦ ❯ ♦ Dedication

What is the driving force behind a project such as this? For Mark and I, our dads played an influential part in introducing us to the wonders of the railroad. Our pleasure continues as I pass on that legacy to my son, Andy, and Mark to stepsons, Josh and Alyc. In part, this book is dedicated to our fathers and sons as a way of saying thanks for sharing our joy.

Yet, as foundational as those forces are, a very special thanks must be given to a mutual friend. He is a consistent encouragement and most valued motivator in the completion of this two-year-long journey from a concept to the written page. That familiar "Busse here" as the phone was answered reminded Mark and I of Dave's availability and patient help. Here's to you Dave Busse! Long live the FP45 in the beautiful Warbonnet red and silver.

◆ ⟩ ◆ Acknowledgement

In the world of color books, a project is only as good as the photographs that support it. How true that is when you consider the nature of the Warbonnet. We had the thrill of poring over hundreds of good photos and the agony of deciding which to include in the book. Happily, we enjoyed both tasks. Many thanks to all who submitted material and made the process difficult. The numerous quality photos submitted helped push the project from a paperback to the hardbound book you hold in your hands.

A special thanks is given to Mike Clayton of Pentrex along with Don Gulbrandsen, Paul Hammond and the fine staff for making this book a reality. Also, the creative work of Katie Danneman and Alan Barrett must be recognized. It was very satisfying to us as authors to know that some of the best in the business were putting our work into print. We hope you enjoy this book as much as we enjoyed putting it together.

Dan Pope
Mark Lynn
Arlington, Texas
September 1994

Foreword

by Michael Gross

"What does the word 'Warbonnet' mean to you?"

Ask that question of the man on the street, and you are likely to be greeted in reply by such names as "Sitting Bull," "Wounded Knee," "General Custer," or even "Tonto." Ask the *aficionado* of rail travel the same thing and, almost without exception, you will hear the name "Santa Fe." Indeed, for the great majority of railfans, as well as that portion of the traveling public old enough to remember, it hardly seems possible to imagine an Atchison, Topeka & Santa Fe Railway without the distinctive Warbonnet paint scheme that has graced its stable of motive power for more than 50 years. That colorful design that sprang from the imaginative brush of a General Motors artist has become a perennial favorite for the railfan community, and is almost synonymous with the railroad itself.

Some are attracted to the mere aesthetics of the Warbonnet, and will wax poetic about line, color, or typeface. Still others are intrigued by the historical context of the design, a splashy descendant of the colorful apparel of the Indian tribes through whose ancestral lands the Santa Fe spawned a group of streamlined *Chiefs*. And a vocal few will argue to the death concerning the design's relative merits as applied to, say, a diesel locomotive manufactured in Schenectady, New York, rather than in La Grange, Illinois.

But whenever I hear the commentaries of the aesthete, the historian, or the "nit-picker," as I listen to their attempts to quantify and objectify, I can't escape the suspicion that, for many of them, this colorful design conjures up more than just ideas: it conjures emotion. And what, after all, should be the surprise in this? If mention of the Warbonnet brings to mind the *Super Chief*, for example, I'd be willing to bet that what many of us remember best, when all is said and done, is not how many F-units were "on

the point" that summer day in 1957, but the cozy, protected feeling we experienced that same night, swaddled in a warm berth, as an electrical storm of Biblical proportions shook the passing Kansas countryside to its foundations. Similarly, if you think of the word "Warbonnet" in the same context as the name "Fred Harvey," I would hazard a guess that the pleasant, warm feeling suddenly washing over you has little to do with the historic significance of that refined gentleman's business association with the Santa Fe Railway. Possibly, very possibly, it has more to do with a distant memory of yourself as a small child, traveling alone, and the special attention you had from a white-jacketed waiter who helped you through the perplexity of ordering for the first time, by yourself, from a dining car menu.

The Warbonnet is more than just a design, more than just a logo: it's a feeling. Some can tell you, in great detail, exactly when and where that feeling began. For others, the context, the occasion, the genesis of that feeling may be too distant, too buried, to recall. For myself, there's never been any doubt. The feeling, the association, is for my grandfather.

He was a Santa Fe railroader for 56 years, and the Warbonnets around which he toiled and upon which he took his travels became, in my mind, inseparable from the happiness he brought to my life. I flew, every summer of my childhood years, to that man's side. And when I flew to him, and to the Mississippi River town in which he lived and worked for all those years, I took flight on the feathers of the Warbonnet. And when he came to visit this little boy in Chicago, it was the Warbonnet, headlight piercing the darkness, easing up to the bumper post at Dearborn Station, heralding the moment when soon, very soon, I would see him stride from the darkened trainshed, emerging from the clouds of trainline steam like an apparition. And while other little boys daydreamed of jousting and dragons and round tables, my castles were the trainsheds and back shops of rail workers—the chivalrous knights of the roundhouse—with my grandpa the lord of the realm.

Memories of that magical man were many, but what I remember most, I suppose, were those long-ago summer nights. After supper, as my grandmother finished drying the last of the dishes, my grandfather and I would stroll the three blocks down to the depot, stake our claim to an idle baggage wagon and, on a hot, sultry, sauna-like summer's night, to the rumble of distant thunder, to the beating wings of moths around the platform lights, to the muffled staccato of the depot teletype, he'd listen, this crown prince of a grandfather, to the dreams of a little boy.

Then, faintly but unmistakably, the sound of a horn. Our ears would strain and, if the wind was blowing in the right direction, we'd hear it again. "He's whistling for Dallas City," Grandpa would say and, in a matter of minutes, a tiny pinprick of headlight would pierce the dark across the river, followed by louder blasts of the horn and the deeper rumble of the train as it started across the Mississippi River bridge. The distant crossing bells, the horn's insistent cries, the glint of headlight through the trees, and, as I inched closer to my grandfather, grabbing for the safety of his hand, there it was: thundering into the depot, smelling of diesel, hot brake shoes, and oil—this red-and-yellow-nosed behemoth, the Warbonnet.

And so, my friend, should we have occasion to meet and talk of the Santa Fe Railway and its colorful livery, try to understand if, in the midst of our discussion of prime movers, or radiator fans, or dynamic brakes, I seem to have drifted away. Forgive me, please, if I appear to be only half listening, if I seem to have retired, suddenly, to some distant, faraway place. I have only slipped away, for one brief moment, to take a seat beside that old man on the baggage wagon . . . with Grandpa, holding my hand, as we watch the Warbonnet go by.

David R. Busse photo

Michael Gross

◆ ❯ ◆ Contents

Authors' collection

Dedication

Acknowledgements

Foreword

Introduction

The Beginnings 1937-1939 .13
Model E1
Inspiration for a Legend: The Story of the *Super Chief*
Amos and Andy
Model E3

The Glory Years 1940-1965 23
Model E6
Models DL-109, DL-110
Model FT
Models PA-1, PB-1
Warbonnets in the Home
Model F3
Model "Erie Built"
Model F7
Model E8m
Self-Propelled Warbonnet Railcars

The Replacements 1966-1973 53
Model U28CG
Model U30CG
Model FP45

A Link to the Past 61
Warbonnets: The New Era
Back to Future with Warbonnets

Third Generation Warbonnets 73
Model GP60M
Model Dash 8-40BW
Model GP60B
Warbonnets in the Desert
Model Dash 8-40CW, Dash 8-41CW
Model Dash 9-44CW

The Future 100

Epilogue 101

All-time Warbonnet Locomotive Summary 102

Introduction

The Atchison, Topeka & Santa Fe Railway Warbonnet design is perhaps the best known, if not the most famous, paint scheme to grace a diesel locomotive. Designed in 1937 by Electro-Motive illustrator Leland A. Knickerbocker, the Warbonnet livery was intended to adorn the sleek new E1 locomotives that Electro-Motive Corporation (EMC) was building for Santa Fe's premier streamliner, the *Super Chief*.

The profile of what appears to be an Indian chief and his flowing feather headdress was developed to accent the Southwest theme that the Santa Fe Railway was famous for promoting. The Santa Fe logo, in brilliant yellow highlighted in black, was stretched out across a sleek, streamlined cherry red nose that flowed back to form an outline of the headdress itself. This distinctive application to the nose of the unit continued along the locomotive's silver sides in the form of a colorful red stripe accented in yellow. It all seemed so perfect in combination.

The sight of Warbonnets racing along the landscape with new Budd-built streamlined stainless steel passenger cars in tow must have startled the train-riding public of the 1930s. The change from black locomotives pulling dark green Santa Fe and Pullman heavyweight cars was so radical, and it happened practically overnight! But no one could argue with the excitement that these famous colors generated—not then and certainly still not now.

The Warbonnet quickly became synonymous with Santa Fe's fleet of high-speed streamliners. Although no one knew it at the time, it was destined to become as legendary as the unequalled quality of passenger service on the Santa Fe. From its beginning as an illustrator's concept of how to coordinate an Indian motif with a sleek passenger train, the famed Warbonnet with all its symbolism continues to represent the cutting edge of rail transportation. Is it any wonder, then, that the Warbonnet is once again at the forefront of Santa Fe's corporate marketing image in the 1990s?

Come with us now as we explore in vivid color that powerful Santa Fe symbol: the Warbonnet.

May 1, 1971, brought a major change to the rail passenger scene in America with the birth of Amtrak (the National Railroad Passenger Corporation). The railroads wanted out of declining passenger business, which was costing them more money to run than it generated. Amtrak was formed by Washington to run a scaled-down schedule of the major U.S. routes. In the early months of the young corporation there was not much change in the power used on the trains, as the railroads paid money or equipment to "join" Amtrak. Even by August 1971, things looked much as usual on the Santa Fe as five Warbonnet-clad F7s are seen gliding down New Mexico's Raton Pass, the highest point on the system, with a combined Super Chief/El Capitan. ***Tom Brown***

The Beginnings 1937-1939

Spurred on by ambitious moves from competitors Chicago, Burlington & Quincy and Union Pacific—both of which were pioneers in the transition from heavyweight, steam-powered passenger trains to lightweight, diesel-powered streamliners—the Santa Fe Railway determined that its future lay as well in the development of streamlined, diesel-powered passenger trains that would capture the nation's attention. As a beginning, Santa Fe ordered two 900 h.p. semi-streamlined box cab locomotives from Electro-Motive. The units had a cobalt blue roof and a darker blue undercarriage, with an olive green body laced in a black-and-tuscan red stripe. These were delivered in November, 1935 accompanied by much fanfare, and the Santa Fe entered the streamline era.

This was only the beginning. In the years following, the major locomotive manufacturers were preparing to offer standardized versions of diesel locomotive models that would revolutionize the look of American passenger trains, and the Santa Fe was interested. Even though Electro-Motive was taking the lead in diesel locomotive development at the time, the other builders—American Locomotive Company (Alco), Fairbanks-Morse (F-M), and Baldwin Locomotive Works (BLW)—were developing comparable technology and products as well. The Santa Fe would ultimately purchase diesel locomotives from all of these companies, but as the transition to diesel took place Electro-Motive would be favored for the majority of the railroad's locomotive purchases.

Facing page: Basking beneath the palms at San Diego, Calif., on Oct. 13, 1948, E1 No. 4 shows off its flashy Warbonnet dress. The "4 Spot" was a part of a two-unit set that consisted of cab unit No. 4L and booster unit 4A. Arriving in April 1938, it was the third E1 set rostered by Santa Fe. The roster pose exposes slight differences in the Warbonnet scheme from that applied to later models, namely an elongated "bonnet" around the first window and the silver half circle around the port holes. The attractive Warbonnet did much to usher in the streamline era on America's passenger trains.
Chard Walker

Richard Gruber collection

Model E1

Builder: Electro-Motive Corporation

"E" for Eighteen hundred horsepower. The E1 was the first in what was destined to become a long line of E-series streamliners from Electro-Motive. Santa Fe's first E-units, the 2A and 2B, arrived on the railroad in May 1937 and, in their Warbonnet colors, quickly made their presence known. The Warbonnet design had been specifically created to adorn these locomotives, and when you consider how perfectly the sleek lines, brilliant colors, and theme of the train matched, you begin to realize the impression Santa Fe wanted to make on the train-riding public.

It was a huge success. The *Super Chief* became the standard to which other streamliners of the time were compared. In fact the 2A and booster 2B set a new record on a promotional run from Los Angeles to Chicago, covering the distance in just 36 hours and 49 minutes for an average 63.9 mph—including stops. Little did anyone realize, though, that the Warbonnets had only just begun making history on the Santa Fe.

Below left: Passing a wigwag signal as it nears Hobart Tower, E1A/B No. 7 powers a northbound San Diegan *toward Los Angeles on Nov. 24, 1949. A Railway Post Office (RPO) car and baggage car are spotted up front on the long holiday consist.* **Ken Douglas**

Below: Westbound at milepost 136 (west of Dearborn Station in Chicago) an A-B-A set of E1s tops Edelstein Hill's 1.2 percent grade near Chillicothe, Ill., with train No. 11, the Kansas Cityan. *Even though the hill may be the hardest pull between Chicago and Kansas City, the three-unit set has no problem with what at one time was a helper district for freight trains.* **Dave Lewis, Steve Rippeteau collection**

Right: San Diegan power—the No. 4 and No. 5 Spot E1As shuffle for position at San Diego in May 1954 between runs north to Los Angeles. The E1s were known to the maintenance shop personnel as the "2 Class" honoring class locomotives 2A and 2B which came first. The E1s were used on the San Diegans *up to and after their rebuilding to E8ms in 1953. They logged a remarkable service record of more than 30 years, from the late 1930s to the E8ms' retirement in 1970.* **Harold Williams, Tom Chenoweth collection**

Inspiration for a Legend: The Story of the Super Chief

here was a time in the not-too-distant past that the train was *the* long-distance travel mode of choice. It was simply expected that a journey of any great distance would be planned by consulting a railroad timetable. If it was travel between major cities that you were planning, you considered the various "name trains" that could whisk you to and from your destination. And if your destination was Los Angeles from the East or Midwest, or vice versa, Santa Fe trains were among those with which you were well acquainted. With Fred Harvey meals and fast, comfortable service—plus a certain allure that hinted of Indians and of the Southwest—the Santa Fe passenger fleet was well-known long before there was ever a *Super Chief*.

This famous train itself had somewhat humble beginnings. Debuting in 1936, the *Super Chief* was the nation's first all-diesel, all-Pullman train, with standard heavyweight Pullmans pulled by a pair of blunt-nosed, semi-streamlined boxcab diesels. Covering the distance between Chicago and Los Angeles in 39 ³/₄ hours, the new train cut 15 hours off the scheduled running time of its forerunner (and sister train), the *Chief*. The two new diesels, nicknamed "Amos and Andy" after the popular radio team of the time, were clocked hitting speeds that topped 102 miles per hour en route!

The railroad's management was excit-

ed about the new train, but realized even before its debut that it would have to take bolder steps quickly. Behind the flashy new diesels, the *Super Chief* was nothing more than a conventional heavyweight passenger train. Competitor railroads Chicago, Burlington & Quincy and Union Pacific had each created media stirs in 1934 when unveiling specially designed streamlined passenger trainsets, and the Santa Fe was determined to do likewise. And rather than just sitting back and letting the various builders come up with ideas, the Santa Fe became involved in the process.

The Santa Fe went on to play an important part in the development of the standard-sized stainless steel passenger car. (Early streamliners such as those pioneered by the Burlington and the Union Pacific had utilized lightweight technology, but in smaller, nonstandard-sized cars semi-permanently joined as sets—thus limiting passenger comfort and operating flexibility.) Working closely with personnel from the Budd Company of Philadelphia—itself *the* pioneer in development of the stainless steel streamlined passenger car—Santa Fe employees strived to make the new trains as modern, yet as distinctively Southwest in flavor, as possible.

April 1936 saw Santa Fe and Budd personnel hammering out plans to bring the whole car concept together. Sterling

Symbols of Santa Fe's—and maybe America's—greatest passenger train, the Super Chief.
Facing page: *An interior view of the Chief's round-end observation car from a Santa Fe brochure.*
California State Railroad Museum collection

Above: *A replica of the distinctive* Super Chief *drumhead.* **Courtesy of Original Whistle Stop**

Right: *A magazine ad touting the Santa Fe streamliner.* **Richard Gruber collection**

"Whe-e-e-ew the New *Super Chief!*"

Just wait, cowboys, till you ride it!
The new Super Chief, all new from head-end to tail sign,
will embody up-to-the-minute rail travel features,
providing the utmost comfort in smooth-riding speed.
The schedule will be new, too!
The Super Chief will depart from Chicago and Los Angeles every day.
This fine all-first-class streamliner
will be one of a whole fleet of new Santa Fe trains soon to be announced.

SANTA FE SYSTEM LINES... Serving the West and Southwest
T. B. Gallaher, General Passenger Traffic Manager, Chicago 4

Santa Fe

The Turquoise Room is located in the lounge car on the new Super Chief, next to the dining car.

You are invited

to entertain a group of your friends privately, en route, in the Turquoise Room aboard the new Super Chief ... the only private dining room on rails in the world. It is one of many features that distinguish this great new train.

Daily service between Chicago and Los Angeles

new Super Chief

Santa Fe

For Turquoise Room reservations, just consult any Santa Fe ticket agent or the dining car steward on the Super Chief.

B. McDonald, whose work on the early Union Pacific streamliners was well-known and who had helped create the paint scheme for "Amos and Andy," headed the design team for the interiors. He had the able help of Roger W. Birdseye, Santa Fe's general advertising manager, who also happened to be well-versed in

Above: A Santa Fe promotional brochure shows the interior of the forward lounge car in the Super Chief *trainset.* **California State Railroad Museum collection**

Left: Ad for the luxurious Turquoise Room dining area on the Super Chief. **Richard Gruber collection**

Southwestern Indian culture. The coordination of the final product was stunning. Gracing the stainless steel fluting on the exterior were such unforgettable names as *Isleta*, *Taos*, *Oriabi*, and *Laguna* (sleepers), *Acoma* (lounge), *Cochiti* (diner), and *Navajo* (observation), taken from various pueblos in Arizona and New Mexico. McDonald and two able Budd architects, Paul Phippe Cret and John Harbeson, created the interior design of the cars—each one unique. Rare woods complemented interwoven fabrics and even sand paintings to emphasize Navajo design and craftsmanship themes. The coordination of the final product was stunning, down to the "Mimbreno" china produced exclusively for the *Super Chief*.

With car production well in hand, the Electro-Motive Corporation of La Grange, Illinois, was forging ahead with the locomotives that would head up the trains. The new E1 diesel locomotive model was taking shape as a futuristic speedster, with a slanting hood protruding from a smooth-sided cab. The body of the locomotive flowed smoothly back in straight lines, creating an impression of speed combined with graceful elegance. This remarkable design would influence the locomotive market for years to come, and the basic lines would be modified in only minor ways to style subsequent models of Electro-Motive's popular E- and F-series locomotives. The Fs would go on to include within their ranks the best-selling diesel locomotive yet produced—the F7.

Working on the paint scheme that would grace the new locomotives was

Leland A. Knickerbocker, a General Motors design stylist. Though his name is not well known today, the work of his hand on "Amos and Andy" is still remembered. As it turned out, his ultimate creation—at least for railfans—was under development with this assignment. Sterling McDonald, who had worked with Knickerbocker on "Amos and Andy," was very confident of the designer's work, yet not even he realized the power of this symbol as it was being pieced together. Emerging from the drawing board was what Knickerbocker described as "the profile of an Indian headdress and the trailing feathers of a warbonnet." The red hood of the E1 formed the figure of a head, with the stylized yellow Santa Fe logo sloping across the sleek nose accented in black. This colorful combination became perhaps the most well-recognized design in passenger train history, and a perfect match for the *Super Chief* cars.

All the preparations of nearly two years of labor were culminated on Saturday, May 18, 1937, as E1A locomotive 2 and its B-unit mate rolled out of the EMC plant at La Grange and backed slowly down the tracks to join the silver cars of the *Super Chief*. As the couplers met, a legend of national significance was born. The powerful imagery and the superior service of Santa Fe's premier passenger train would go on to become synonymous with the railroad itself. The mystique that was created still lingers today.

If image is everything, then the Santa Fe Railway has it all.

Amos and Andy

Rebuilt: Topeka (Kansas Shops), AT&SF Ry.

Perhaps the most unusual of all locomotives to wear the famous Warbonnet colors were the rebuilt versions of Santa Fe's first diesel streamliners, which had been delivered to the railroad in 1935 by Electro-Motive. Dubbed "Amos and Andy" by admirers, the two locomotives were rebuilt in Santa Fe's Topeka, Kansas, shops in 1938, emerging with several mechanical and cosmetic changes. The most noticeable of these were the reconfiguring of the front ends with elevated cabs and a curved sheet metal nose that looked more like an English Bulldog than a sleek streamliner, and application of Warbonnet colors, unmistakably Santa Fe in any case. Six-wheeled trucks replaced the original four-wheeled ones to reduce "hunting" of the wheels at high speeds.

The two locomotives remained unique up to the date of their retirement, and additionally required above-average amounts of maintenance to keep fit. Complaints about them were few, however; after all, these were the first streamlined diesels on the railroad. As such they were held in high regard by crews which had learned about the new diesel technology working with them.

The 1-Spot Amos and Andy rounds the curve bringing train No. 12, the Chicagoan, *into Lawrence, Kan., in July 1945. The unique rebuild with its face-like features leads part of what Santa Fe declared to be at one time "America's Largest Fleet of Streamline Trains." Trains 11 and 12, the* Chicagoan, *and its counterpart the* Kansas Cityan, *were regular assignments for these locomotives through the 1940s.*

Model E3

Builder: Electro-Motive Corporation

The E3 was next in the succession of EMC's efforts to refine its successful E1 model that had been introduced in 1937. The E3 was equipped with two 1,000 h.p. V-12 model 567 engines that combined to yield a total of 2,000 h.p., an improvement over the 900 h.p. of the old 201A engines. The new model also came with many more interchangeable parts and major components built by Electro-Motive itself, instead of by outside suppliers such as General Electric, which had supplied earlier EMC locomotives with components.

The highly successful use and testing of Electro-Motive demonstrator 822 by the Santa Fe led to an order, and E3 A- and B-unit set 11 was delivered to the Santa Fe in the spring of 1939. It was to be the only one of its kind on the railroad.

A- and B-unit set No. 11 was the only E3 delivered to Santa Fe by Electro-Motive Corporation. It arrived on the property in spring 1939. The E3A is shown at Lawrence, Kan., on Dec. 26, 1955. The locomotive had amazing longevity, working on the railroad for nearly three decades. **Robert P. Olmsted, R.R. Wallin collection**

The Glory Years 1940-1965

With the introduction of its fleet of stainless steel stream-lined trains such as the *Super Chief* and *San Diegan* head-ed up by sleek E1s proudly wearing Warbonnet colors, the Santa Fe soon became recognized as an industry leader in providing high-quality accommodations and timely service for its patrons. The railway's reputation was unequalled among the riding public, leading to an upswing in patronage on premier trains and necessitating orders for more streamlined cars and locomotives to handle the business.

Who could argue with first-class Harvey House meals and service, with the luxury of the Turquoise Room and the Pleasure Dome Lounge, or with the *Super Chief*'s reputation as America's classiest streamliner between Chicago and Los Angeles? And who could dispute the allure of Santa Fe's classy Warbonnet design in adding to that reputation? As a symbol the Warbonnet had few peers, and its powerful imagery became synonymous with the Santa Fe itself. Its impact as a marketing milestone was even felt in the toy industry, bringing the Santa Fe emblem literally into the homes of thousands of Americans.

Facing page: Train No. 12, the Chicagoan *with expanded daily service from Chicago to Oklahoma City, Okla., and Dallas/Ft. Worth, Texas, makes a station stop at Topeka, Kan., in April 1954. Its beautifully clad Warbonnet E6A is followed by an E8B and E6B. Topeka has always been an important stop on the Santa Fe as evidenced by the railroad's Topeka Shops that have been involved in locomotive repair dating to the late 1870s. The gradual enlargement of the shops over the years makes it presently the largest shop complex on the whole system.* **Clayton Tinkham**

Authors' collection

Model E6

Builder: Electro-Motive Corporation, Electro-Motive Division

The standardized version of the 2,000 h.p. model E3. The E6s had the same V-12 model 567 engines as the E3, and were known as the "11 Class" due to their close relationship to Santa Fe's one-and-only E3, number 11. The first E6 diesel locomotives on the railway were acquired in May 1940. By 1941, the Santa Fe had a total of four E6 A-units and two B (or booster) units on the roster.

Above right: E6A/B No. 13 idles in Dallas Union Station near the scene of one of the most infamous crimes in U.S. history. It is Dec. 8, 1963, just two weeks after John F. Kennedy was assasinated, and the Texas School Book Depository Building (with the large Hertz sign) looms in the background. The location of the alleged sniper's nest is the second window from the top on the right corner of the building. **Dick Kuelbs**

Right: Number 15, the last of the successful E6As to join the Santa Fe roster, poses at Topeka, Kan., in December 1957. The old Chevy truck and Railway Post Office (RPO) car to the left lend an added touch to this vintage view of the classic streamliner. **Tom Chenoweth collection**

Opposite: In October 1958, Emporia, Kan., hosts train No. 5, service from Kansas City to Galveston, Texas, with E6A No. 13 on the point. Many railroads had contracts with the Postal Service to carry the mail—the main purpose of this train, as evidenced by the abundance of head-end cars. **W.A. Gibson Jr.**

Model DL-109 / DL-110

Builder: American Locomotive Company

The first attempt at a streamlined diesel locomotive by the American Locomotive Company (Alco) incorporated distinctive styling. The famous industrial designer Otto Kuhler was responsible for its unique lines, but this model was never given much chance to catch on due to wartime restrictions that were imposed on Alco's output (indeed, on all locomotive builders) shortly after its introduction. As with EMC's model E3 and E6 locomotives, these Alco passenger units were each powered by two 1,000 h.p. diesel engines.

Alco locomotives 50A (model DL-109) and booster 50L (model DL-110) were delivered in 1941 with much fanfare, just before imposition of wartime restrictions. It quickly became apparent that the model 539 engines powering these locomotives were better suited to flatland running rather than heavy mountain grades, so this unique team ran out their service lives for the most part in the Midwest where heavy grades were few.

Opposite page top: *An interesting broadside view of the front end of DL-109 No. 50 brings out the smooth lines of this Kuhler designed carbody. Notice as well the six-wheel Alco trucks that add the feeling of speed and a streamlined appearance. The photo was taken at Kansas City, Kan., in December 1958.* **W.A. Gibson Jr.**

Opposite page bottom: *Unique on the Santa Fe roster, No. 50 DL-109 and booster DL-110 show off their version of the Warbonnet scheme in a sunny pose at Kansas City, Kan., in June 1959. The second lower headlight was a modification added later to produce better visibility for safety reasons. This change caused the Santa Fe name to be written twice within the nose oval creating a disappointing alteration to the original Warbonnet application.*
Ray Lowery

Art, Richard Gruber collection

Every inch the Chief

Yes, *Little Chief*, our Chief measures up to the name!
For it is the all-Pullman, extra-fare, transcontinental streamliner (along with the daily Super Chief) that is famous among discriminating travelers for smooth-riding speed, roomy comfort, and delicious Fred Harvey meals.

The Chief provides daily service between Chicago and Los Angeles, Chicago and Phoenix, Chicago and San Diego.
In conjunction with the New York Central 20th Century Limited, the Pennsylvania Broadway Limited, and Baltimore & Ohio Capitol Limited, it provides daily Pullman service between New York and Los Angeles, and between Washington and Los Angeles without changing cars.

Santa Fe

SANTA FE SYSTEM LINES... Serving the West and Southwest
T. B. Gallaher, General Passenger Traffic Manager, Chicago 4

Model FT

Builder: Electro-Motive Division

Although earlier diesels had brought a new image to the Santa Fe, the FT, first introduced in 1939, truly changed the face of the entire railroad. Steam began to give way to diesel power, especially out west where it had always been difficult to keep thirsty steamers supplied with adequate water due to the lack of suitable natural supplies on the surface. Although designed specifically for freight service by builder Electro-Motive, optional higher-speed gearing to make the FT suitable for passenger service was available.

Santa Fe Railway ultimately owned the largest fleet of FTs. As part of its last delivery, one 6,000 h.p., four-unit set was painted in freight colors yet geared for higher speeds and equipped with steam generators to supply heating and air-conditioning for passenger service. Tests on the new set were successful; the four-wheel trucks with greater weight on drivers proved better suited to mountain grades than six-wheel-trucked locomotives, which often required helpers. Between April and August 1946, Santa Fe converted ten sets—each with two cab units sandwiching two booster units—of FTs for passenger use and repainted them in Warbonnet colors.

Below left: A clean Warbonnet dress adorns the No. 165 FT set parked outside the Barstow, Calif., diesel shops in August 1947. For the most part the FTs were operated as four-unit sets and had a drawbar link between A and B units rather than a regular coupler. The remarkable FTs' performance convinced railroads that diesel power was the way of the future. **Ken Douglas**

Below: A rare look at FTs on the San Diegans *is presented by FT No. 168 and B-unit booster on the train at San Diego, Calif., in May 1954. The half set is unusual as the locomotives usually operated in four-unit sets. In fact, the model was first offered by Electro Motive only as a four-unit set with an inseparable drawbar. Modifications and further testing showed AB sets could provide enough power to get the job done on shorter trains, and not tie up a complete four-unit set when extra power was not needed.* **Harold Williams, Tom Chenoweth collection**

The late afternoon sun greets FT set No. 159 in shining red, yellow and silver paint leading the first section of train No. 24, the Grand Canyon, *as it rounds the curve near old Cajon Station, Calif. The assault of Cajon Pass lies just ahead as the streamliner continues its trek toward Chicago. Often when railroads had a large surge of riders for a particular date and train, it was broken and sent in "sections" close together to keep the schedule instead of a lone long train that was harder to handle. This was the case many times with a secondary train such as the* Grand Canyon, *an all-coach train with no sleepers. This scene was recorded on Sept. 16, 1948.* **Chard Walker**

High in Cajon Pass, Calif., in January 1967, the snow-capped San Bernardino Mountains form a scenic backdrop for a train load of railroad enthusiasts riding behind a pair of Alco PAs headed for Barstow, Calif. Number 68 and mate emerge from the tunnel at Alray in beautiful sunlight pulling the old heavyweight cars.
Alan Miller

Model PA-1 / PB-1
Builder: American Locomotive Company

The American Locomotive Company (Alco) re-entered the stream-lined locomotive marketplace after the conclusion of World War II, hoping to compete with industry giant Electro-Motive, which had gotten a firm hold on customers during the years of wartime restrictions. Both freight and passenger streamlined diesels were produced by Alco, but the Santa Fe sampled only the passenger models. Ultimately, the railroad owned a total of 28 A-units and 16 B-units produced to these designs.

The distinctive styling of Alco's streamlined passenger locomotives was first witnessed on the Santa Fe in 1946, when a three-unit A-B-A set, numbered 51, 51A, and 51B, was delivered to the railway following display at New York's Grand Central Terminal September 22-24. While there, special ceremonies commemorated the fact that the 51 was Alco's 75,000th locomotive. With their 2,000 h.p. 16-cylinder model 244 engines, each of these locomotives matched the horse-power ratings of the Electro-Motive E3 and E6 models, but with only one instead of two engines providing the power.

Above right: Two PAs sit at Houston Union Station with train 66 in June 1966. Number 57 and sister will lead the early evening departure to Temple and Brownwood, Texas, to combine with a train from Fort Worth and San Angelo, Texas, for a connection with the San Francisco Chief *at Clovis, N.M.* **Dan Pope collection**

Right: PAs 77 and 74 idle on the point of a San Diegan *ready to depart for L.A. in December 1955. The PAs were the primary power on the Surfliners from the late 1950s to the mid-1960s. Two units seem a bit too much power for this train, but tight schedules and the poor mechanical reliability of the Alcos required an extra unit in case of problems.* **Dan Pope collection**

Model PA-1 / PB-1

Builder: American Locomotive Company

Facing page: PAs No. 74 and No. 67 stoke it up as only PAs could as they ready themselves at Redondo Junction in Los Angeles for what was then thought to be their last use on the L.A.-to-Chicago run of the Grand Canyon, *in December 1967.* **Alan Miller**

Above: Perhaps the most unusual application of the Warbonnet dress was that which adorns PA No. 53 as it idles in L.A. on February 13, 1960. The gold, blue and silver alterations were given to commemorate a General Electric special. **Alan Miller**

Above right: The chill of a December day challenges crews servicing PA 74L as it stops in Shopton, Iowa (Fort Madison), with westbound No. 23, the Grand Canyon, *in 1967.* **S. D. Rippeteau**

*Like better-known Warbonnet-clad EMD units, the red-and-silver PAs were also featured in print advertisements promoting Santa Fe passenger trains. **Authors' collection***

Warbonnets in the Home

Below: The box cover of American Flyer's 3/16-inch scale PA/PB set adorned in the Warbonnet scheme. Today, these models are a much-sought-after collectors' item.
Authors' collection

The public popularity and eye-catching colors of the Warbonnet were not overlooked by others. In fact, the classic silver, red, and yellow design was, and still continues to be, perhaps the most widely used diesel paint scheme produced by toy and model railroad manufacturers.

The Santa Fe was approached by none other than Joshua Lionel Cowen, founder of Lionel Toy Trains, who was seeking assistance in reproducing the popular F3 locomotive model. By 1948, Lionel diesels entered the toy model market featuring the Warbonnet scheme, complete with a set of silver streamlined cars. Although Lionel also brought out a New York Central diesel train set featuring the NYC's gray Lightning Stripe scheme, the Santa Fe diesels stole the show—and the market—year in and year out. It has been said that the Warbonnet was responsible for Lionel's phenomenal postwar success, contributing to the company's strong establishment as the toy train leader. And the Warbonnet diesels are still being produced today!

A year later, Lionel's chief competitor, American Flyer, brought out a beautiful Alco PA / PB set in 3/16-inch scale. As collectors' items, these locomotives are very much sought after today. The saga is complete when you realize there is hardly a toy train or scale model manufacturer that has not marketed some version of Santa Fe's Warbonnet scheme—right up to the modern Dash 8s and other locomotives of today. Amusement park railways also found the scheme popular with children and adults alike. How could anyone resist riding behind such colorful locomotives?

No. K5374W $71.50

AMERICAN FLYER LINES 470   AMERICAN FLYER LINES 471   AMERICAN FLYER

Super long and super powered . . . .

AMERICAN FLYER LINES 470   AMERICAN FLYER LINES 471   AMERICAN FLYER

No. K5375W $71.50

TWO *American Flyer* "CHIEFS"

• Two motors • Air chime whistle • Knuckle couplers • 3/16" scale

26

Right: Destination Chicago and Dearborn Station! Sporting the famous red, yellow and silver paint with a matching train in tow, the No. 24 A-B-B-A F3s negotiate the maze of switches leading into the depot. The old Erie freight house on 14th Street lines the tracks on the east, hosting some classic boxcars. The view here is timeless as another Santa Fe streamliner arrives from the west coast on June 28, 1959. **Robert P. Olmsted**

Model F3
Builder: Electro-Motive Division

The year 1946 brought the introduction by Electro Motive of its new model F3 locomotive, a modernized and uprated version of the model FT. The F3 offered 1,500 h.p. in contrast to the FT's 1,350 h.p., and ultimately a total of 23 four-unit sets (A-B-B-A) would proudly display the famous Warbonnet colors of the Santa Fe.

F-units would go on to become the most prolific of all first-generation diesel power in America. As the era of steam drew to a close on the nation's railroads in the late 1940s and early 1950s, so too did the first generation of diesel locomotive design which included all types of streamlined diesel locomotives.

Above right: The fast moving Super Chief *is spotted near Victorville, Calif., in full stride with green flags flying. With F3 set No. 22 leading the way across the desert, the train is headed for Barstow and its next station stop. Who could argue with clean Warbonnets on the* Super Chief *being the American passenger train experience at its best?*
Frank Peterson, Alan Miller collection

Right: A classic scene beneath the palms at Riverside, Calif., in 1949 finds a four-unit set of F3s pausing for a station stop. Santa Fe received most early model cab type diesels in four-unit lots when taking delivery. These were usually two cab units and two "B" or booster units and these were given a single number as in this case No. 17 LABC. These units then usually ran together. Number 17 LABC was the second set of F3s delivered to the Santa Fe, in November 1946. ***K.B. King Jr.***

Model F3

Builder: Electro-Motive Division

Facing page: A headlight pierces the darkness at the Los Angeles Union Passenger Terminal which is the end of the line for Santa Fe passenger trains coming into L.A. Nightfall finds F3 AB No. 33 resting in between runs on the San Diegans in August 1970. The time honored pastime of watching trains is being carried on by a father showing the streamline beauties to his son. **Dan Pope collection**

Right: A "Del Mar Race" special zips past the quaint depot at San Juan Capistrano, Calif. carrying riders to the track at Del Mar just north of San Diego. A siding and wye at the racetrack made it very convenient to the race goers who were virtually dropped off at the front door. F3 No. 21 and train will lay over to escort the fans home after a day at the horse races. The date is Sept. 30, 1966. **Clayton Tinkham**

Model "Erie Built"
Builder: Fairbanks-Morse & Company

Locomotive builder Fairbanks-Morse (F-M) entered into large-scale diesel locomotive manufacturing just prior to the close of World War II, when demand for diesels to replace steam locomotives was about to reach its high point. The company's locomotives were unique in that they were powered by opposed-piston diesel engines, rather than the in-line and Vee engines which remained standard with other major locomotive builders at the time.

Unfortunately, the unique engines on F-M's locomotives were mechanical orphans on most railroads, and for this reason the company's locomotives were not always well-received by the crews that had to work on them.

The sole representative of streamlined Fairbanks-Morse passenger locomotion on the Santa Fe was a three-unit (A-B-A) set which was known by the model nickname "Erie-Built" since the builder had never given it any other designation. The set, numbered 90, 90A, and 90B, was delivered to the Santa Fe in June 1947. The unusual model designation was rooted in a manufacturing contract between F-M and General Electric; since F-M was swamped with orders at the close of WWII, arrangements were made to have streamlined F-M freight and passenger locomotives assembled at the GE plant in Erie, Pennsylvania, for a time.

Opposite top: *The No. 90 Erie-Built set leads the second section of train No. 24, the* Grand Canyon, *just west of Victorville, Calif. It is April 10, 1949, and the unique set looks brand new. Due to their unreliability on the long transcontinental trek, the Erie Builts were soon given assignments that kept them close to home and under mechanical supervision.* **Chard Walker**

Opposite bottom: *In May 1953, at San Diego, the No. 90 set pauses in between assignments on the* San Diegans. **Harold Williams, Tom Chenoweth collection**

Right: *Inbound near Mission Tower, the Erie Builts bring a train home to Los Angeles Union Passenger Terminal, circa 1953. Santa Fe mechanical personnel labored to make the F-M set more dependable for passenger power, but the opposed piston design seemed better suited for applications such as stationary power plants and tugboats. The set was sent to General Electric in 1963, 16 years after coming to the Santa Fe.* **Ken Douglas**

Model F7

Builder: Electro-Motive Division

With the production of the model F7 locomotive, Electro-Motive reached what many consider to have been the high point of streamlined, enclosed carbody diesel development. The sales and production figures support this belief, as the F7 was the best selling cab unit-type diesel locomotive model in history. Although the 1,500 h.p. Fs were designed principally for merchandise service, Santa Fe took advantage of their adaptability, eventually making them the backbone of the railway's passenger locomotive fleet.

The first F7 set, numbered 37L, 37A, 37B, and 37C, was delivered to the Santa Fe in September 1949. Additional orders brought the total to 101 F7s rostered for passenger use. Unlike with earlier models, where locomotives were kept in specific sets for the most part, Santa Fe took more liberty than ever before in breaking F7 sets up depending on specific need—a usage pattern which would eventually become standard practice. The F7 would go on to become the locomotive model that best symbolized the Warbonnet paint scheme, perhaps because of the large number rostered by the Santa Fe—and perhaps also because of this locomotive's universal popularity among railfans.

Top and right: It is May 1970 and Amtrak is only one year away as F7 328A departs Dearborn Station in Chicago with the San Francisco Chief. ***Fred Matthews***

Above: Warbonnet F-units dominate the scene at Kansas City Union Station in June 1969. Near the headhouse a trio of F7s await departure while, at left, what appears to be another F7 is really F3 No. 27 fitted with F7 grilles. ***Dan Pope collection***

Model F7
Builder: Electro-Motive Division

Facing page: The Grand Canyon *crests Edelstein Hill as it makes its westward trek across Illinois in February 1971. Train No. 23, led by F7 No. 343, is working its way out of the Illinois River Valley en route to Galesburg, its next stop.* **Steve Rippeteau**

Top: In California's Tehachapi Mountains, a five-unit set of F7s rolls through Caliente with No. 2, the San Francisco Chief, *in April 1967. Santa Fe's route to San Francisco was not the most direct, but excellent service and a timely schedule made it an attractive alternative to competing roads.* **Alan Miller**

Right: Three years later, in April 1970, four F7s lead the westbound San Francisco Chief *through Holt, Calif.* **Tom Brown**

A special train chartered by National Railway Historical Society (NHRS) in November 1969 has photographers scattering after recording the unique consist paused at the large depot at Pueblo, Colo. The well-known landmark, in a city known for its steel production, dates back to its construction in 1889. The station and yards were operated by the Pueblo Union Railway and Depot Company to serve the four railroads that ran passenger service into the "Steel City." The Denver-bound special is handled by Santa Fe's veteran E8m No. 84 and an F7B pulling a colorful string of passenger cars from the Rio Grande and Union Pacific. **Ed Fulcomer**

Model E8m

Builder: Electro-Motive Division

Santa Fe's small fleet of E8ms were actually the old E1s—those famous first-bearers of the Warbonnet paint scheme—after being upgraded to more modern standards. In 1952, with more than two million service miles on each of their old 201A diesel engines, numbers 2 and 4 were traded in to EMD at La Grange, Illinois. What Santa Fe got in return were E8 carbodies with all new parts, except for the main generators and trucks from the E1s.

Eventually, all of the older E1s were converted, with the last unit delivered in May 1953. The Santa Fe was pleased with these locomotives but the E8s would nevertheless work out their years of service mostly on secondary routes and less-than-first-class trains.

Above: The white classic depot at Dallas, Texas, is a fancy backdrop to E8m No. 87 and B-unit mate during a station stop on a hot afternoon in August 1967. Number 87's train is part of the through service from Chicago that came off train No. 15, the Texas Chief. *Cars bound for Dallas were switched out at Gainesville, Texas, 86 miles to the north and made into train No. 115 for the trip into "Big D," while No. 15 came up from Houston by way of Ft. Worth on the way back to Chicago, with No. 116 making the connection to Gainesville.* **Dick Kuelbs**

Something new to

remember

every magic mile

There's so much to see... so much to do... so many comforts to enjoy, that you'll never forget your trip through the colorful Southwest on any one of Santa Fe's five famous trains between Chicago and California

Santa Fe

Super Chief - Chief - El Capitan
Grand Canyon - California Ltd.

R. T. ANDERSON, General Passenger Traffic Manager, Santa Fe System Lines, Chicago 4

Richard Gruber collection

Model E8m

Builder: Electro-Motive Division

*The massive trainshed and stationhouse of Kansas City Union Station dwarf the Santa Fe streamliner sitting in its shadow. The beautiful structure dates from 1914 and was once the center for passenger train activity in a city known for its railroads. It is summer 1966 and although business is not what it used to be, E8m No. 87 and two B-units with 2,000 h.p. each make ready for departure. The upgraded 567 engine with its added horsepower made these popular speedsters mechanically appealing. While not having the aesthetics of their E1 ancestors, the E8s were dependable motive power that ran until their retirement one year short of Amtrak's debut in 1971. **Keith Ardinger***

Top right: A country grade crossing near Lawrence, Kan., provides a perfect vantage point to observe new locomotives. E8s led by No. 87 and assisted by an E6B, haul train No. 11, the Kansas Cityan, *out of town. The July 6, 1953, date means the No. 87 is only four months old, yet it is proving itself worthy of wearing the Warbonnet as it performs its faithful duties. The old 1947 Pontiac "8" in the foreground brings back memories when cars had a personality all their own.* **©1992, Wallace W. Abbey, all rights reserved**

Right: Former E1, the "7 Spot" is now E8m No. 85. The rebuilt unit and two boosters ease a Santa Fe streamliner into Topeka, Kan., over the Kansas (Kaw) River bridge. A heavyweight RPO car is part of today's consist. It is August 1967 and the E8s are nearing the end of a fine career. In 1970 they will be traded in to EMD for freight power. It is hard to believe that America's passenger train industry is winding down and Warbonnet dressed steramliners will soon be gone.* **Tom Chenoweth collection**

Self-Propelled Warbonnet Railcars
Builder: Electro-Motive Corporation and Budd Company

Four self-propelled railcars would eventually wear the Santa Fe's Warbonnet colors, although none of the four began their careers in the famous scheme.

Two of Santa Fe's early gas-electric "doodlebugs" were so graced fairly late in their service lives. Delivered by EMC in June 1931, the M-160 initially burned a gas distillate to turn a generator supplying electric power to traction motors—hence the term "gas electric." This was the case as well with cousin M-190, otherwise nicknamed the "Old Pelican," delivered to the Santa Fe by EMC in 1932. The gas electrics performed well in branchline passenger service, and were an important link in the railroad's transition from steam to diesel.

In December 1949, the M-190's distillate engine was replaced by a model 567 V-12 diesel engine and Warbonnet colors were applied. The M-160 was given a similar treatment in October 1952, except that the new engine was a model 567 V-6

Top: Photographers show up to greet Santa Fe's only RDC pair as they unveil their new Warbonnet dress in late June 1957. The year before, a major derailment of the RDCs in San Diegan service killed 30 people. Although the accident was proved to not be the fault of the units, Santa Fe management, along with the State of California, were not convinced that the RDCs were repaired and banished them to a low-priority run between Newton and Dodge City, Kan. The pair served there until 1965 when they were elevated to name status again by taking over the El Pasoan service which ran from El Paso, Texas, to Albuquerque, N.M. **W.A. Gibson Jr**.

Left: A head-on shot of RDC-1, No. DC-191 reveals its Warbonnet face as interested onlookers inspect the unit at Topeka, Kan., on June 21, 1957. **W.A. Gibson Jr**.

diesel. These upgrades showed Santa Fe's commitment to the railcars. It was less expensive to upgrade than to buy new power, and the doodlebugs were sturdy units. Remarkably, both survive today.

Another unique self-propelled railcar model to sport the Warbonnet scheme was the RDC-1. The designation RDC stands for Rail Diesel Car, a product of the Budd Company of Philadelphia. A pioneer in early diesel streamliner manufacture, Budd became famous for the design and production of stainless steel streamlined passenger cars, which would become the company's real staple. The RDC was an attempt by Budd to revive the "doodlebug" (self-propelled railcar) market with stainless steel streamlining and diesel propulsion.

The two RDC's purchased by Santa Fe in 1952 were conventional factory models seating 90 passengers each. The railroad planned to use them to supplement *San Diegan* service with additional runs, and they performed this duty with two daily runs until 1956. Initially, the units were not painted in the Warbonnet scheme, but by 1955 they both sported red-and-silver. Unfortunately, a tragic derailment of the RDCs killed 30 people in early 1956, and the pair was banished from California to lower-priority runs in Kansas, Texas, and New Mexico. One of the two was rebuilt into a combination passenger-baggage configuration following the wreck, reducing seating capacity but better adapting the RDCs to their new service.

Top*: The Warbonnet-clad M-160 is spotted at Clovis, N.M., in December 1964, more than 33 years after it started service for AT&SF. It was the first doodlebug on the railroad to be rebuilt and though the new innards extended its life, it was still a rolling museum piece by 1964. M-160 and cousin M-190 carried on the important tradition of branchline passenger service that brought the outside world to those off the beaten path. In its later years the M-160 was the most popular equipment for the train between Clovis and Carlsbad, N.M.* **Tom Chenoweth collection**

Above*: The M-190 in storage at Clovis, N.M., in November 1969. "Old Pelican," came to the Santa Fe in 1932 and carried a 900 h.p., Model 194 gas distillate engine, one of two ever built. It had an articulated carbody and baggage space behind the engine room. Santa Fe wanted to use the M-190 to power a five-car train from Kansas City to La Junta, Colo., but the unit proved unreliable. Before its repowering in 1949, the M-190 spent most of its time hauling short trains between Amarillo and Lubbock, Texas.* **K.C. Henkels**

◆ 3 ◆

The Replacements 1966-1973

By the mid-1960s, the mainstays of Santa Fe's Warbonnet fleet were showing their many years of hard service. Breakdowns were becoming more common and maintenance costs were rising. Although very much aware that passenger train travel was on the decline, the Santa Fe was not willing to compromise its high standards of service. The only solution was to buy new passenger locomotives.

There were problems with this solution. The only units offered by the various builders at the time were essentially freight units, with a steam generator added as an afterthought to supply heating and air-conditioning needs for passenger service. The aesthetics of these non-streamlined designs did not appeal to Santa Fe management, and the builders were asked to submit proposals for new passenger locomotive models. Due to immediate needs, however, Santa Fe took delivery of ten General Electric freight units with steam generators while continuing to press for new designs. By 1967 both EMD and GE had delivered new locomotives to the railway, designed and intended for passenger service.

Facing page: Dearborn Station in Chicago was the eastern terminus of Santa Fe's transcontinental route. In a city known for its passenger trains, Dearborn was the first of the Windy City's large stations to be built, dating from 1885. In March 1970, things are not quite what they used to be, but the afternoon sun lights up a trio of GEs, with U30CG No. 405 at the forefront, waiting to depart from beneath the trainsheds at Dearborn. **Reid McNaught**

Authors' collection

Model U28CG

Builder: General Electric

The year 1960 marked the first production of road diesel locomotives by builder General Electric. Since the 1930s, the electrical giant had been building small switching locomotives on its own, and supplying traction motors, generators, and other electrical equipment to the American Locomotive Company (Alco) for application in its various road diesel locomotive models. (The term "road" as used here basically distinguishes larger locomotives intended for service on mainline and shortline common-carrier railroads, as opposed to the smaller models generally employed on industrial or switching lines.) The GE-Alco partnership ended in 1953, when General Electric began development of its own line of road diesels. The first of these came in 1960.

By the mid-1960s, when Santa Fe was looking for newer power to replace its aging passenger locomotive fleet, GE sought to provide the answer: the U28CG. Featuring a 2,800 h.p. 16-cylinder engine housed in a road switcher-type carbody and riding on three-axle trucks, this model was also equipped with a steam generator. As such, Santa Fe took delivery of ten units in 1966 for dual-service use on passenger and freight assignments, decked out in the famous Warbonnet colors. Unfortunately the U28CGs enjoyed only a brief time in Santa Fe passenger service; following derailments in which they and their U30CG cousins were implicated as part of the cause, the ten locomotives in this class were reassigned and regeared for freight service in 1969.

Top right: *Dirty, but faithful to the task, lone U28CG No. 353 hustles a five-car* San Diegan *through Commerce, Calif., and past the Lever Brothers complex, in January 1969.* **Todd Novak collection**

Right: *A view from the steps of Tower No. 55 in Fort Worth, Texas, reveals a train from San Angelo, Texas, with U28CG No. 357 in charge. Train No. 16 is headed northbound and is about to cross the Texas & Pacific main line, then veer to the left on its way to the depot. The short four-car consist is typical of train 78 as it treks into Fort Worth to make connections with the* Texas Chief. **K.B. King Jr.**

Although Santa Fe's premier transcontinental trains the San Francisco Chief, Super Chief *and* Chief *were handled by the sleeker-looking EMD Fs, the GE-built U28 and U30CGs found their niche on the likes of the* Grand Canyon *and* Texas Chief. *Such is the case this fall day in September 1968 as a trio of GEs are photographed easing the westbound* Grand Canyon, *train No. 23, through Kansas City, Kan., on its path to Los Angeles, Calif. The dusty-looking U28CG twins upfront—No. 353 and No. 355—offer a dirty contrast to their shiny new cousin and remind the onlooker of a passenger scene that is long gone.* **K.B. King Jr**.

Model U30CG

Builder: General Electric

The second of General Electric's contributions to the Santa Fe passenger fleet was somewhat more aesthetically pleasing than the first had been, but the six model U30CGs delivered to the Santa Fe in 1967 would nevertheless remain the only ones of their kind ever produced. The distinctive feature of this locomotive model was its tall, fluted stainless steel sides, which in combination with Warbonnet colors made for a striking, if somewhat unconventional, appearance.

Designed for dual passenger-freight service, these locomotives were at first assigned to the *Grand Canyon Limited* and later to *San Diegan* service. As with their U28CG cousins, the U30CGs unfortunately enjoyed only a brief time in the passenger spotlight. Following a tragic derailment at speed in Illinois, both of these GE models were regeared and reassigned to freight service after they were found to have contributed to the derailment.

Top right: *It's May 1968, after the U30CGs' arrival on the Santa Fe, and Nos. 400/402 still have a like-new appearance. The Santa Fe took great pride in the clean look of its passenger fleet right down to fresh silver paint on the pilot and underbody, even if it meant a bit of overspray from the car department. The Warbonnet pair prepares to leave Fort Worth, Texas, on the westbound* Texas Chief *headed for Houston and an 8 p.m. arrival.* **Tom Hughes**

Right: *U30CG 404 has drawn freight duty in March 1969 as it makes a brief stop in Chillicothe, Ill., for a crew change before it continues its westbound run.* **S.D. Rippeteau**

Santa Fe's slow train to the coast was the Grand Canyon. *The westbound version is seen paused at Chillicothe, Ill., with the U30CG class unit No. 400 and cousin U28CG No. 358 in matching Warbonnet dress idle in the lead as passengers make final boarding. The heavyweight "baggage" car and lack of domes give away the secondary status of this mostly coach train.* **R.T. Smart**

Model FP45
Builder: Electro-Motive Division

Santa Fe continued strong in the second-generation diesel market to reinforce its commitment to the passenger train. This was in contrast to nearly all other railroads, which were shying away from anything having to do with passengers. In fact, the railroad world was somewhat surprised when EMD's new FP45 was introduced and nine units delivered to the Santa Fe in late 1967. Numbered 100 through 108, these units looked as though they had been styled specifically for Santa Fe's Warbonnet dress.

The lines of this model were in some ways a radical departure from the earlier, rounded styling of Es and Fs, yet the similarities were apparent as well. Technologically, there were major changes in the structure of the new model; the term "cowl" would eventu-

ally be coined to describe the locomotive's hood or covering, which was not a structural part of the frame—unlike Es and Fs which utilized the sidewalls as a part of the locomotive frame structure. Inside was a 20-cylinder, 3,600 h.p. model 645E3 engine and a steam generator.

Well aware of the downturn in the rail passenger market, the Santa Fe at the same time was pioneering the development of high-speed freight service. The FP45s would perform well in "Super C" service which began in early 1968, as well as any other assignment which called for speed and style. Well-received from the start, the FP45s were promptly assigned to handle Santa Fe's flagship, the *Super Chief.*

Left: *Although primarily purchased to bring new life to an aging passenger fleet, the FP45s were really dual-service units. Santa Fe's high speed raceway between California and Chicago did more than just move people, it was the channel for excellence in high speed freight and merchandise movement. To accent that fact the Santa Fe inaugurated the* Super C, *the world's fastest freight train. Its advent on Jan. 17, 1968, brought a record breaking run from Chicago to Los Angeles in 34 ¹/₂ hours. Its contract to shippers guaranteed 48-hour service between Chicago and the coast. With renumbered red-and-silver FP45 No. 5944 and blue Nos. 5920 and 21 in control, the westbound* Super C *train No. 128 races through Streator, Ill., with a string of piggybacks holding tight on the curve in July 1972.* **Steve Rippteau**

A view into the maze of tracks that make up Chicago's Dearborn Station reveals FP45s 100 and 103 this hazy day in August 1968. The cowl units are preparing to pull out with a Santa Fe westbound headed for Los Angeles 2,222 rail miles away. The look into Dearborn tells us it is not the temple of transportation it used to be—though the oldest station in Chicago it will close with the coming of Amtrak. The owner of the station, Chicago & Western Indiana, had Alco RS-1s that performed much of the switching for the station tenants. A black-and-yellow C&WI unit is seen on the left with the engineer shouting instructions to the Santa Fe crew. The perch for the photographer is the Roosevelt Road overpass, a favorite location for those wishing to record the Windy City rail scene because it ran by not only Dearborn, but La Salle Street Station, Grand Central Station, and Union Station. **William White**

The cosmetically restored Fs are seen at Summit, Calif., during a taping session on Feb. 10, 1989. The units were not made operable for the filming sessions and were therefore pushed by a pair of freight units (barely visible around the curve). The finished tape was distributed to shippers to promote Santa Fe's Quality services and was very well received in the industry.
Elrond G. Lawrence

◆ 4 ◆

A Link to the Past

In spring 1988, preserved F7A 347C and sister B-unit 347B were repainted from the "Yellowbonnet" colors that they had worn in their latter years of freight service on the Santa Fe. Using stencils saved from the trash bin by a painter in the San Bernardino shops, the classic red, yellow and silver Warbonnet scheme was again applied to these two lucky survivors. The reason? The two units were part of a representative, historic collection of Santa Fe locomotives—both steam and diesel—that had been stored in the Albuquerque, New Mexico, roundhouse in anticipation of the eventual start-up of a Santa Fe Railway museum.

When it had become apparent in the 1980s that such a museum was not to become a reality, this collection was donated to the California State Railroad Museum in Sacramento. The entire col-

lection would be moved to Sacramento as a group, but even before the collection could be moved the question was being asked: could the two Fs be painted back into their Warbonnet colors? A group of determined volunteers started a fundraising effort to cover the costs, and the Santa Fe Railway agreed that the units could be painted "at cost" in San Bernardino.

February 1989 saw the units returning to Southern California as stars in a video aimed at Santa Fe shippers. This video linked the railway's modern, premium freight services to the standards that Santa Fe passenger trains of the past had been famous for. The repainted Warbonnets were used to head up a complete, sparkling stainless steel passenger trainset as the "link to the past" in the presentation. As it turned out, this was a harbinger of things to come.

The unpowered, but externally restored, Warbonnet F-units glide through Cajon Pass east of Alray in February 1989. With the freight units providing motive power out of sight, it was easy to imagine that the Super Chief *had been brought back from nearly two decades of oblivion.* **Elrond G. Lawrence**

Numbers 100, 101, and 102 pose on Cajon Pass on Aug. 10, 1989. The 100 had just been released from the paint shop and the three were together for the first time for a publicity train. The train was posed at several of the prime photo locations in the pass for company photographers.
David R. Busse

Warbonnets: The New Era

Former Santa Fe President Michael R. Haverty was the man responsible for the rebirth of the Warbonnet paint scheme in the late 1980s. In the following letter, Mr. Haverty was kind enough to share his recollections of how it all took place.

◆ 〉 ◆

Above: Michael R. Haverty who, while president of the Atchison Topeka & Santa Fe Railway, was instrumental in reviving the Warbonnet image.
Photo courtesy Michael R. Haverty

Top right: *The primary change in the new Super Fleet Warbonnet scheme was a bold, red* SANTA FE *on the sides of the locomotive—styling that better advertised the railroad, and was quite well received even by AT&SF purists.* **Dan Munson**

Bottom right: *Santa Fe used its newly resurrected Warbonnet image to promote the Super Fleet concept in a variety of places—for example on a billboard visible from southbound Interstate 29 in Kansas City in August 1990.* **Dan Munson**

Back in April 1988 when I was vice-president, operations of the Santa Fe Railway, we took an inspection trip with a group of rail analysts. I was standing on the platform in Albuquerque, New Mexico, admiring our train which was made up of several stainless steel passenger cars, business cars, and three freshly washed blue-and-yellow locomotives. It was reminiscent of the *Super Chief* except for the lack of the Warbonnet paint scheme on the locomotives.

I had been thinking about how we might bring back the Warbonnets for some time. It just seemed to me that we were not taking advantage of the most famous, highly recognized paint scheme ever for a railroad locomotive. The Warbonnets were synonymous with the *Super Chief* and the *Super Chief* was a standard of quality. The *Super Chief* was Santa Fe's flagship in the passenger train days and I knew our employees took a great deal of pride in it. I felt if we could bring back the Warbonnet paint scheme we could recapture that pride and also have a

With the power of over a hundred new locomotives, we're aiming for the stars.

To be the highest quality transportation company on earth, we set our sights considerably higher.

That's why this year Santa Fe is adding 123 of the most sophisticated new locomotives ever built to our Super Fleet of trains. Each features beautiful red and silver colors in our famous Warbonnet design.

These are super-powered, super-engines. With wider cabins and micro-computers on board. They're built with more muscle and less weight, to travel at higher speeds with greater fuel efficiency. And starting today, they'll be pulling our freight light years ahead.

We also added 40 new locomotives to our Super Fleet last year in our traditional blue and yellow design.

All these new engines embody Santa Fe's devotion to providing the fastest and most reliable transportation you can get. A devotion that with our fleet, grows bigger and stronger every day.

To find out more, call Santa Fe Intermodal at 1-800-825-1660, or Santa Fe Commodities at 1-800-TRY-ATSF. Because a railway that reaches for the sky, is bound to cover a lot more ground.

Santa Fe Super Fleet
Setting the track record in transportation.

The Atchison, Topeka and Santa Fe Railway Company. 80 E. Jackson Boulevard, Chicago, Illinois 60604-2401
©1990 The Atchison, Topeka and Santa Fe Railway Company

Atchison, Topeka & Santa Fe Railway Company

highly visible symbol for advertising and marketing programs. I decided standing on the platform at Albuquerque that someday I would paint our locomotives with the old red-and-silver Warbonnet scheme. Mike Martin, our public relations representative from Los Angeles, was also on the platform and I told him of my desire. Since Mike is a railfan, he naturally thought the idea was great.

Mike told Homer Henry about what I said. Homer was on my staff at that time and he also became excited about the idea. Homer researched the idea with the locomotive manufacturers.

Below: A Super Fleet special was stopped at Sullivan's Curve to allow company photographers to make photos from a variety of angles. Railfan photographers, alerted to the event by the very active grapevine in southern California, were on hand in force to document the occasion for themselves. In one bold stroke, the Santa Fe had opened the doors for a wave of positive publicity and renewed employee pride. The show had just begun. **Alan Miller**

Above: Sunrise on Aug. 24, 1989, finds the 100 on the point of the Q-LANY1-23 east of Flagstaff, Ariz., at milepost 335. The QLANY train is Santa Fe's Quality service train operated in conjunction with Conrail from Los Angeles to New York. The "1" in the train symbol indicates that this is the first section of the train, while the "23" indicates that it left its point of origin on the 23rd of the month. For the first several months after their new paint jobs, the 100s could usually be found on this and other premium intermodal trains between California and Chicago. **Mark R. Wayman**

Above: When the first new Super Fleet locomotives, the GP60Ms, were delivered in May 1990 they were assigned to the 100 class. Subsequently, the FP45s were renumbered to the 90 class. Number 91, the former 101, is shown in San Bernardino, Calif., on May 23, 1990, during its first run in the new number. **David R. Busse**

Left: The 104 leads a doublestack train east near the Camp Cajon road crossing on Nov. 15, 1989. The rear of the train is passing Blu Cut—named for the color of the rocks—the location of the infamous San Andreas Fault. Santa Fe recently contracted with an earthquake research laboratory to get up to the minute, accurate information when an earthquake does occur. This will allow the railroad to resume normal operations more quickly than in the past, when the entire line over the pass had to be shut down and inspected fully after a quake. **Randy Keller**

Unfortunately, carrying two different paint schemes on locomotives is not inexpensive, so not everyone was as enthused as I was about reviving the Warbonnet scheme. While Homer continued to prod me about putting the new paint scheme on 1989-authorized locomotives, I told him the timing was just not right.

In May 1989 it was announced that I would be made president of the Santa Fe on June 1. Homer told me that if I wanted the 60 locomotives from GE and the 63 locomotives from EMD that were to be delivered in the near future to be painted in the Warbonnet scheme, a decision would have to be made immediately. Since I was the new president, I felt the timing was not only right but also that I didn't need anybody's authority to do it. I told him to go ahead and advise all concerned of the decision and that it had my blessing.

Homer had a model made up of the paint scheme (which I still have) that had Santa Fe shown on one side in the old style and on the other in the more modern bold lettering. I chose the bold lettering in red. We had eight FP45s that I authorized to be painted in the new Warbonnet paint scheme to show everyone what we were doing and to begin using in advertisements.

I decided that we would use Warbonnets on our high-speed intermodal trains because they were the most highly publicized and because the new locomotives were four-axle, high-speed units designed for intermodal service. I told Vice-President, Public Relations Bob Gehrt that we would call our new locomotives "Super Fleet," an obvious play on words of *Super Chief* and *Super C*, the world's fastest freight train during John Reed's tenure. Bob suggested we just refer to all of our trains as the Super Fleet. I agreed.

I felt the timing was right for the rebirth of the Warbonnet scheme as I wanted it to coincide with the rebirth of the Santa Fe. I wanted to return Santa Fe to its former position of prominence and to again make it a standard of excellence synonymous with quality. We began using that theme in our advertising and promotional material. The rest is history. I can only tell you that the Warbonnet recognition and value exceeded my wildest dreams. We received millions of dollars in free advertising as it again became the most recognized locomotive paint scheme in the world. Even model trains returned to the Warbonnet. It became one of the biggest marketing coups in recent history. It put Santa Fe back in the news and, more importantly, helped the company regain its image as a quality carrier along with some fundamental changes in attitude about what the customer wanted. It is an achievement that I will always be proud of.

Although this has been a rather lengthy explanation of how the Warbonnet trademark was brought back, this is the first time that I have taken to sit down and write the history of what happened.

Mike Haverty

Below: Just like the old days of Santa Fe passenger trains! FP45 Nos. 100 and 101 idle with the five-car special late at night in AT&SF's Glendale, Ariz., piggyback yard near Phoenix. In the morning this will become the first Warbonnet passenger train to call at the Grand Canyon since 1967.

can still remember the "oohs" and "aahs" that perfect July morning in 1989 when the two FP45s paused for photographers at Sullivan's Curve in Cajon Pass. The light was exquisite and the dozen piggyback cars behind the locomotives looked great. Cameras clicked incessantly.

Two of us that morning had seen these same FP45s 20 years earlier, brand new, in their original red-and-silver livery leading the *Super Chief/El Capitan*. That was an era of retrenchment in the passenger business and Santa Fe's new FP45s were about the only positive development as passenger trains dwindled. Within four years of their delivery, Amtrak took over Santa Fe passenger service and the FP45s got freight assignments and blue paint.

That morning in 1989, Amtrak had been synonymous with passenger trains for almost two decades. For some of us, these spotless FP45s evoked memories of Dearborn Station in Chicago, of blue-jacketed porters next to *Palm*-series sleepers, of Turquoise Rooms and Big Domes, Fred Harvey, John S. Reed, Santa Fe French Toast, Hi-Level chair cars and late-night meets at Barstow. They were a link to the old days of Santa Fe passenger trains, and we left Cajon that day with more than just exposed film. We promised ourselves to pursue the link to the past. If Santa Fe ever ran a passenger special with these red-and-silver steeds in charge, we would be there.

In July 1989, Santa Fe management decided to paint all eight remaining 5990-

Warbonnets

Text and photography by David R. Busse

class FP45s into the new Warbonnet scheme, and to adorn a new order of freight units with the "new" look. For the next eleven months, until the delivery of the new GP60Ms, the venerable FP45s wore their original 100-class numbers and were once again the leaders of the fleet. Every event that warranted a special Santa Fe presence across the system drew an FP45, and in between performances they were usually found leading the railroad's hottest freights. They powered several short passenger specials in California promoting trash-by-rail schemes, a bond issue to fund commuter rail, and even pulled the *Rose Bowl Special* from Los Angeles to Pasadena on New Year's Day.

But the magical, "back-to-the-future"

assignment for the Warbonnet FP45s happened in April 1990, when units 100 and 101 led a five-car consist from Phoenix, Ariz., to the south rim of the Grand Canyon—reviving a company tradition that ended when passenger service to the canyon ceased in 1967. The train was a Santa Fe "party" for customers attending an intermodal freight conference, and was made possible by the 1989 reincarnation of the Santa Fe Grand Canyon Branch by the new Grand Canyon Railway.

We first laid eyes on the consist in the darkness of April 3, 1990, as the train sat under heavy guard in the railway's Glendale, Arizona, piggyback yard. A gruff-looking railway policeman understood why we wanted to take photographs

Above: The Grand Canyon Special arrives at Williams, Ariz., and the ex-Santa Fe, now Grand Canyon Railroad, depot.

Below left: The special stops at Ash Fork, Ariz., to allow a Winslow-based crew to take over.

Below right: The special passes through the scenic Hassayampa River Canyon, just outside of Wickenburg, Ariz., on the Phoenix Subdivision.

Above: A going-away shot near Mattie, Ariz., reveals the Santa Fe *business car on the rear.*

Right: *Business car attendant Anthony Phillips, a 29-year veteran of the railroad, poses next to his charge at Grand Canyon, Ariz., on April 4, 1990. Phillips worked the last Santa Fe special to the Grand Canyon in 1966.*

Back to the Future with Warbonnets

at midnight and graciously allowed it.

The next morning, Santa Fe Passenger Extra 100 took the main under gloomy skies. A light rain fell as the train passed Castle Hot Springs and snaked along the Hassayampa River. Approaching Matthie, the sun came out. Most fans would envy the passengers that morning, yet witnessing the Warbonnet FP45s in the desert made us at trackside feel like a privileged lot. At Ash Fork, a Winslow-based train crew took over in a scene that looked like one from the late 1960s.

When the special reached Williams and the Grand Canyon Railway, there were banners flying and officials on hand to meet the train. The presence of a real Santa Fe passenger train in front of the beautifully restored Harvey House snarled downtown traffic. Williams is a town where most of the population really did understand how special the event was.

The train continued up the Grand Canyon line and arrived at the South Rim in late afternoon where it met the southbound Grand Canyon train pulled by 2-8-0 No. 18. As the steam train left, the stage was entirely Santa Fe's. The AT&SF depot, spruced up after years of neglect, still wore the company logo and looked much as it did when the last Warbonnets called here. Tour buses, Fred Harvey Company "Harveycars," pulled up to meet the train as Fred Harvey buses had done since the turn of the century. And it all took place in the shadow of the stately El Tovar Hotel, the Santa Fe-built lodge that is still *the* place to stay at the canyon.

Passengers left the train, posed for pictures, said their good-byes and boarded buses for the airport. A dozen or so rail-

fans continued to take pictures. It was difficult to leave. Some of us who had not been here since the glory days muttered, ". . . the place hasn't changed a bit."

Within a month, the new 100-class Warbonnet GP60Ms began arriving from EMD and the FP45s were renumbered into the 90-class. Most high-profile passenger assignments became the domain of the new Super Fleet Warbonnets.

By 1994, the FP45s were in the general freight pool, and future passenger assign- ments were unlikely. After their retire- ment, hopefully one of these steeds will be enshrined in a place of honor like the California State Railroad Museum. And though preservation would save the Warbonnet FP45s for future generations, there will never be a time quite like that afternoon in April 1990. There are some experiences in life that you wouldn't trade for all the Kodachrome in Rochester. Thank you EMD, Leland Knickerbocker, John S. Reed and Mike Haverty.

This high desert scenery is typical of the Grand Canyon branch. The special approaches Valle, Ariz., a former cattle shipping point on the branch line.

◆ 5 ◆

Third Generation Warbonnets

When the Santa Fe began streamlining its operations in the late 1980s by eliminating many en route crew changes, it became apparent that some basic changes had to be made with locomotive cabs to maintain an environment conductive to safety. Santa Fe had been a pioneer in equipping locomotives with cab air-conditioning, but this was not enough. Crews needed a less-fatiguing workplace to stay alert on the longer runs, and additional protection from collisions. Other railroads and the major U.S. locomotive builders GE and EMD were also involved in solving the same problems.

Santa Fe began its search for ideas in Canada, where a cab design with added collision posts and extra insulation, among other features, was in use on the Canadian National Railway. After several months of negotiations with U.S. Customs officials, a CN locomotive was allowed to make one Chicago-Los Angeles round trip for evaluation. Train crew members were asked to inspect the locomotive during extended stops at each crew change point along the way. Santa Fe's mechanical department, armed with a long list of suggestions, then approached the locomotive builders.

What emerged from EMD bore a strong external resemblance to the FP45 cab of the 1960s. The resemblance ended there, however, as inside it was a different story. Ergonomically designed seats, a clean cab with fewer protrusions, a console setup for the operating controls instead of the traditional control stand, and thick layers of insulation to combat noise and vibration were just some of the many improvements over predecessor locomotive cabs. The application of Warbonnet colors set the new units apart from the rest of the Santa Fe fleet in splendid fashion. With delivery of the first GP60Ms in May 1990, a new era had begun.

Above: *Santa Fe officials preparing to ride a special behind the FP45 91 pause as the GP60M 100 leads its first eastbound trip past their train at San Bernardino on the morning of May 23, 1990. This side-by-side view allows a comparison of the noses of the 1960s-era cowl unit with the 1990s-era wide-nose safety cab.* **David R. Busse**

Facing page: *Some spectacular vistas can be had in the big country of west-central New Mexico. The afternoon sun glints off the windshields of five GP60Ms running "elephant style" on the Q-NYLA as it passes the signals and hotbox detector at milepost 65.8, west of Quirk. The five units have their train well in hand as they make the long climb to the Continental Divide 65 miles to the west.* **Bryan Moseley**

Model GP60M

Builder: Electro-Motive Division

Above: While many people were awed by the Warbonnet scheme worn by the GP60Ms, the model was perhaps more significant because it was the first on the Santa Fe equipped with EMD's crew comfort cab. This interior shot of GP60M No. 115 shows the desktop-style control console used by the engineer. **Ken Fitzgerald**

Left: The bright red nose of GP60M 161 contrasts nicely with the snow and trees as the 991 train roars out of the east end of Abo Canyon at Scholle, N.M., on Dec. 29, 1990. The engineer has his charges in throttle notch 8 as the train climbs the 1.25 percent grade and prepares to enter the 15-mile-long section of two-track CTC to Mountainair, where Abo Summit will be attained. **Steve Todd**

Late on the afternoon of Nov. 11, 1990, the 199 train approaches the I-25 overpass at milepost 2 just west of Belen, N.M. As always, the 199 is made up entirely of articulated equipment for a maximum efficiency in train handling and fuel consumption. Santa Fe was a pioneer in the use of articulated spine cars, starting with the 10-pack Fuel Foilers in the 1970s. Now equipment like this is common from coast to coast. The four GP60Ms led by the 114 will blast up the 1.25 percent grade up to Dalies (the start of which can be seen near the rear of the train) in short order. **Bryan Moseley**

Model GP60M
Builder: Electro-Motive Division

Right: A warm Feb. 26, 1992, finds a pair of GP60Ms leading the S-LAZJ1-24 out of Cleburne, Texas, on the last leg of its trip from Los Angeles to Zacha Junction, formerly Santa Fe's Dallas intermodal terminal. Cleburne, once the site of the shops that produced, among other things, Santa Fe's fleet of CF7s, no longer sees through traffic from the West Coast. Most of this traffic now travels to Fort Worth via Union Pacific's Baird Subdivision, then swings northward to Santa Fe's new Alliance intermodal yard north of Fort Worth. **Mark R. Lynn**

Lower right: Twisting through the narrows at Victorville, Calif., No. 100 is in full cry as it assaults the east slope of Cajon Pass with a stack train on January 19, 1992. Only a year and a half old, the unit has already passed the quarter million mile mark in demanding high-speed service. **David R. Busse**

Facing page: An early snow frosts the Iowa landscape as the 144 steps onto the west end of the Mississippi River bridge at Fort Madison at 11:44 a.m. on Nov. 8, 1991. This is the 991 train, and the crew will be in Chicago, 232 miles distant, in time for supper. As soon as the rear of his train rounds the curve on the Illinois end of the bridge, the engineer will advance the throttle on his console and his train will be rolling at 70 mph in a matter of minutes. **Mark Zaputil**

Model Dash 8-40BW
Builder: General Electric

The 4,000 h.p. Dash 8-40BW was locomotive builder General Electric's first contribution to the growing Warbonnet-painted Super Fleet. Nearly as long as the six-axle SD40-2 of competitor EMD, these big four-axle GE units dominate the scene whenever they appear with other types of units. With delivery of these locomotives, GE has managed to overcome any negative feelings Santa Fe may have harbored about the less-than-stellar careers of the C30-7s, GE's previous model produced for the railroad. In fact, the Dash 8s, as they are known for short, are popular with both management and crews.

In all, 83 Dash 8-40BWs from two orders now ply Santa Fe rails. The first order of 60 units was delivered during October and November 1990, while 23 more were delivered in March and April 1992. The second order featured a slightly different cab roof profile so as to clear coal loaders along the system, and the horsepower rating was decreased to 3,800 from 4,000 h.p.—this latter change actually beginning with the final 20 units of the first order.

The odd-numbered units, which are not equipped with event recorders, were delivered first. Even-numbered units do have these devices and GE preferred to keep them separate during construction. The GE "Super Cab," as it is called, bears little resemblance to its EMD counterpart. The slope of the "cheeks" is different and headlight placement is centered, not offset. Number boards are mounted above the windshield to maintain consistency within the Santa Fe fleet, instead of being mounted next to headlight as has been specified by several other railroads with GE Super Cab units.

Right: Dash 8-40BW 501 is framed in the ivy-covered archway at the San Bernardino depot as it pauses for one last crew change before the last lap into Hobart Yard in Los Angeles. **Mark R. Wayman**

Facing page: The helpers have just cut off an eastbound freight at Frost, Calif., as a westbound led by three Dash 8s starts to dig in on the east slope of Cajon Pass. The westbound faces a 16-mile climb to Summit with a maximum grade of 1.8 percent. **Elrond G. Lawrence**

Model 8-40BW

Builder: General Electric

Left: The morning of Feb. 16, 1992, dawned cold and raw in the high desert town of Mojave, Calif. Snow clouds hang low over the Tehachapi Mountains as Dash 8-40BW 536 leads a matched set of GEs under the signal bridge a couple of miles east of town. A few of the thousands of windmills that dot the east side of Tehachapi Pass can be seen to the left of the locomotives. **David Rector**

Above: The cabs of GP60Ms and Dash 8-40BWs are quite different externally, but inside there are a lot of similarities as this view of the 503 attests. The controls and their layout are quite similar between the two models, simplifying the job of crews who must operate both. **Ken Fitzgerald**

Right: Just a month into its career, Dash 8-40BW 533 passes Santa Fe Junction, in the shadow of downtown Kansas City on Dec. 8, 1990. **Dan Munson**

Snow is fairly common near the top of Cajon Pass during the winter months, although it usually doesn't last long. The morning of Jan. 8, 1992, finds the 159 leading an eastbound piggyback train through fresh snow less than a mile from the summit. This train has come up the south track, which was the original track over Cajon. It features some stretches of 3 percent grade, and is usually used by westbounds descending the hill. **James A. Speaker**

Model GP60B

Builder: Electro-Motive Division

For several years in the 1980s, Santa Fe Railway experimented with modern-day B-units, rebuilding SD45 and SD45-2 cab-equipped locomotives into cabless B-units in its own shops. But when Santa Fe announced that its 1991 locomotive order would consist of 20 EMD GP60Bs, observers quickly recalled the A-B-B-A consists of red-and-silver Warbonnet F-units from days gone by. Since FRA missile-proof glass does not have to be maintained along with many other items in a locomotive cab, B-units offer cost savings over cab-equipped locomotives, although operational flexibility is sacrificed.

The GP60Bs were intended for use on intermodal trains, which generally run from point to point over long distances without any switching involved en route. In this type of service, locomotive consists generally do not undergo changes either, and Santa Fe felt that the savings realized over the life of the units would offset the inherent reductions in flexibility. The GP60Bs have performed as intended in this service, and Santa Fe tries to have two cabbed units facing forward on each train to minimize delays in the event any problems develop with the lead unit. As such, classic A-B-B-A locomotive sets, prized by photographers, are rare.

Above right: *It's unusual to find any kind of B-unit by itself, but here's the 326 at Dallas, Texas, waiting to be placed in a consist for the next trip west. If you look closely, you can see that the fuel tank was moved forward slightly on the GP60Bs to help distribute the weight of the unit evenly.* **Mark R. Lynn**

Right: *A summer thunderstorm is brewing over the Rio Grande Valley as an A-B-A set of GP60Ms enters the west end of Abo Canyon in central New Mexico on Aug. 31, 1992. The hillside the photographer is on is one of the great places on the Santa Fe to watch and photograph trains, as you can see almost all the way into Belen, 20 miles to the west.* **Ken Fitzgerald**

The American Southwest, stretching from the Texas Panhandle through New Mexico, Arizona and into southern California, seems to represent the spirit of the Santa Fe. In many people's minds, the region and the railroad are synonymous.

Warbonnets in the Desert

Text and photography by Dan Pope

The powerful symbolism of the Warbonnet has been well documented. Its resurrection is testimony to its enduring popularity and national appeal. Each day, red-and-silver locomotives highlight the roadbed running between the metropolitan centers of Chicago, Los Angeles, Houston and Kansas City, in the process brightening the scenery at lesser-known burgs such as Ft. Madison, Iowa, Raton, New Mexico, Victorville, California and Crowley, Texas.

It is a common opinion that the American Southwest, stretching from the

Left: Dash 8-40BW leads a short intermodal train into the west end of the Winslow yard on March 5, 1994. After a short stop for a crew change the eastbound will continue its trek across the Arizona desert.

Texas Panhandle through New Mexico, Arizona and into southern California, seems to represent the spirit of the Santa Fe. In many people's minds, the region and the railroad are synonymous. Even in the days of Santa Fe steam, the marketing gurus played to the culture of this territory with passenger train names such as the *Chief*, the *Super Chief*, the *Grand Canyon* and the *Scout*. Yet names were not enough to communicate the true flavor of the region and with the advent of the diesel came the explosion of color. Isn't that what makes the Warbonnet scheme so appealing, no matter what model wears it? The Warbonnet colors and composition paint the perfect portrait of this rugged territory and all it represents; and Warbonnets in the desert must be seen in person to fully understand the both the spirit of the region and the railroad.

Invitations are opportunities! The chance to visit the main line through the high desert of Arizona could not be passed up. I had never witnessed the red-and-silver locomotives in the days before Amtrak, but this would be my occasion to photograph the modern-day Super Fleet at those often-heard locations of Williams Junction, Flagstaff and East Darling. These would be the settings for my memories, my turn to experience Warbonnets in the desert.

The first weekend in March brought the promise for clearing weather with plenty of snow on the peaks of the San Francisco Mountains. My cold weather gear was packed, should a late winter storm hit—it seemed that whatever the weather I would not be disappointed. Having checked into Flagstaff the night before after a two-hour drive from Phoenix, the next morning brought that deep blue cloudless sky and a chill in the air that told me this trip was going to be all I had hoped for.

Destination: Winslow, Arizona. Early morning in the desert on a highway overpass at the west end of Winslow's yard provided a great vantage point to witness a set of Dash 8-40BWs gearing down for yard limit speed. The workday for the crew in the 569 was ending after a long night pushing this hot shot down the road from the last crew change at Needles, Calif. The daybreak chase from Flagstaff had paid off as the desert background of brown earthy hues paid perfect compliment to the red and silver traversing the barren terrain. The snow-covered San Francisco Mountains provided a perfect backdrop to the arid scene. The stop at Winslow was short-lived; the next crew was waiting to board at the yard office. With the trade-off complete, No. 569 and its mates notched it up, moving their time-sensitive commodities closer to delivery.

Below: Winter still has a grip on the Arizona divide as a quartet of Dash 8-40CWs pass with a 198 train in early March 1994.

Right: Santa Fe's QNYLA races past Darling, Ariz., behind Warbonnet Dash 8-40BW No. 517.

Evidence of a late winter storm covered the ground at the Arizona divide just west of Flagstaff. The heat of the early afternoon continued the melt off, making for soggy conditions. Even here on the high desert it can become a winter wonderland. I was waiting on westbound train No. 198. The train symbol revealed its priority status: 1 for Chicago, its origin, 8 for Los Angeles, its destination, and the middle number 9 meaning hot, hot! As I mused on that information my feet reminded me that standing in this melting snow was becoming unpleasant. Had my blood thinned that much since I left my Chicago roots to move to Texas? Finally, the sound of diesels echoed around the bend. Wow, what a sight, a perfect matched set of Dash 8-40CWs in control. The snow in the foreground set the Warbonnets in a postcard setting against the deep blue sky and pine trees. Cold feet or not, it was worth the wait.

My pulse quickened as I steadied myself on a small knob of ground and peered through the lens, looking down into the valley that hosted the 1.4 percent grade on this ribbon of track at Darling, Ariz. "Hot rail!" came the call. Santa Fe's hottest train, the QLANY (2nd section), had just popped out of the pine woods and was snaking through the crossovers and under a signal bridge, seemingly gathering momentum for the for the half-mile uphill climb to my location at milepost 329. With black exhaust billowing out, No. 517, a Dash 8-40BW, leaned into the curve creating the definitive "in your face" pose. This was mainline railroading at its finest and what better way to highlight it than to have a Warbonnet leading the way.

The barren sections of Santa Fe's line relocation west of Williams Arizona are miles from nowhere and accessible only by Forest Service roads. This section of rail was completed in 1961 to bypass the stiff grades between Ash Fork and Crookton. Our rented four-wheel drive had proved up to the task of getting us to

the desired locations. This was true desert railroading. A high green on the signal bridge west of West Perrin gave the clue that an eastbound was due. A set of Warbonnets would be the preferred power to accent this desolate setting of green junipers, burnt brown clay and cut rock cliff. My desire became reality as another set of GE Warbonnets rounded the curve in splendid fashion. The NYK stacks were headed for Chicago where they would be handed over to Conrail for the remainder of the their transcontinental voyage. But for now they were part of a timeless scene only possible on Santa Fe's desert railroad.

There is something very inviting about the warm, yellow late afternoon light in the desert, and from a photographic standpoint it is the prime time of the day. This was my last day on the desert and time was winding down on my window of opportunity. The scanner was silent as we sat on a bluff in the warm sun near West Perrin. The facing signal behind us was dark as we waited out the last minutes of day. The light faded as the sun sank, but wait . . . another check of the signal showed high green. Listening carefully, the stillness of the desert was broken by the sound of diesel engines around the curve. Could it be— yes—a Warbonnet followed by three blue-and-yellows on a stack train. Dash 8-40CW No. 837 seemed to glow in the prime light, the trees behind gave the appearance of a scene out of some model railroad magazine. But this was no model, it was the real thing. What more could I ask for to end the trip in grand fashion?

How do you put the experience of a trip like this in words? It is better told in images that evoke the emotions of having been there in person to witness the passing of a symbol that goes beyond the excitement of the moment. It is being able to trace a thread of history from an Arizona hillside in 1994 to Leland Knickerbocker's drawing board in 1937. My front row seat in the desert made it easy to drift back to a time when Warbonnet-clad PAs and Fs were the standard of power on Santa Fe's fast trains—a proud tradition that the Super Fleet Dash 8s and GP60Ms carry on today as Warbonnets in the desert.

Left: A set of General Electric Warbonnets leads a train of NYK stacks eastward at West Perrin, Ariz.

Right: Bathed in the golden hues of sunset, the 837 is the lone Warbonnet leading an eastbound intermodal train at West Perrin on March 4, 1994.

A trip like this is better told in images that evoke the emotions of having been there in person to witness the passing of a symbol that goes beyond the excitement of the moment. It is being able to trace a thread of history from an Arizona hillside in 1994 to Leland Knickerbocker's drawing board in 1937.

Third Generation Warbonnets 89

Model Dash 8-40CW

Builder: General Electric

In announcing its 1992 locomotive order late in 1991, Santa Fe Railway included six-axle locomotives for the first time since 1983, when the last C30-7s were delivered by GE. With doublestack intermodal business increasing rapidly and a new coal-hauling contract close at hand, the railway's need for a large group of units capable of efficiently handling these slower, heavier trains was apparent. Santa Fe's SD45 locomotive fleet, six-axle mainstay of the railroad for many years, was past its 25th birthday and, in spite of being rebuilt in the early 1980s, gulped fuel at a high rate with its 20-cylinder engines.

Both Electro-Motive and General Electric competed to win this large locomotive order, but the contract was ultimately awarded to GE for construction of 67 safety cab-equipped, 3,800 h.p. Dash 8-40CWs. Union Pacific, Conrail, and CSX were already amassing large fleets of these heavy-duty units, and railroad photographers eagerly awaited their appearance in Warbonnet colors. The faithful were not disappointed. With the last of the order, delivered in early November 1992, the units can be found all over the system—usually on the heavy trains they were intended to pull.

Top: Dash 8-40CW 816, a unit from the 1992 order, leads a 189 train westward at Yampai Summit, Ariz., on June 20, 1993. ***Mark R. Wayman***

Above: The 842 poses at Saginaw, Texas, on July 10, 1992. ***Mark R. Lynn***

Right: Number 915, part of the second order of 3,800 h.p. Dash 8s, leads a J.B. Hunt trailer train at Bazar, Kan., on June 27, 1993. ***Mark R. Lynn***

Model Dash 8-40CW
Builder: General Electric

Left: The demise of the Pasadena Subdivision—once synonomous with the Warbonnet-led Super Chief—has made this scene impossible to repeat. Dash 8-40CW 918 is shown leading an eastbound Wilmington Turn, heavy with K Line containers, at Glendora, Calif., on Jan. 3, 1994. Just weeks later, all through trains were rerouted to the San Bernardino Sub, and the trackage through Pasadena began its transformation into a light rail line. **James A. Speaker**

Above: The first revenue run for the 800s was the S-CHLA1-15, a Chicago-Los Angeles train. They had been received from Conrail at Streator, Ill., a few days earlier and delivered to Kansas City, where they were inspected and made ready for service. They were placed on the train at Kansas City the afternoon of April 15, 1992, and are seen climbing past Cosnino, Ariz., late the next day. **Mark R. Wayman**

Right: The image of today passes the image of yesterday as Warbonnet 824 overtakes blue-and-yellow SD40-2 5072 at Cajon Summit in August 1992. Santa Fe hasn't dropped the old scheme—and units are still repainted blue and yellow—but the last new road units not delivered in the Warbonnet scheme were 1988's Dash 8-40Bs. **Randy Keller**

Model Dash 8-41CW

Builder: General Electric

With traffic on the rise, Santa Fe was still hungry for reliable power, leading to the decision to purchase more six-axle locomotives in 1993. General Electric again won the bidding war and was rewarded with an order for 60 more Dash 8s. These 4,135 h.p. units, classified as Dash 8-41CWs, were slated for delivery between March and June 1993. Before delivery of this order was complete, Santa Fe announced the purchase of 25 additional C41s, bringing the order total to 85 units. The last unit of the original order, the 925, and all the units in the second 1993 order received split cooling radiators. The lower the inlet air temperature in a diesel engine, the better the fueling efficiency, so air from the turbocharger is cooled before being introduced to the cylinders. The spotting feature for the aftercooler is that the wing on the radiator section is slightly thicker at the outside edge than the wing on units not so equipped. The 951 was the last of the Dash 8-41CWs to be delivered, arriving in November 1993.

Top: The 945, generally described as a Dash 8-41CW though basically a 4,135 h.p. Dash 8-40CW, at Dallas, Texas, on Dec. 14, 1993. **Mark R. Lynn**

Right: A Dash 8-41CW leads a westbound stack train at Rana, Calif., on Nov. 11, 1993. **David Miller**

Facing page: Minutes after a crew change at Belen, 930 leads a hot TOFC train east at the mouth of Abo Canyon at Sais, N.M. **Brian Solomon**

Model Dash 8-41CW

Builder: General Electric

Facing page: On the evening of Jan. 23, 1994, Dash 8-41CW 940 leads a westbound into the setting sun at Danby, Calif. **Brian Solomon**

Left: Santa Fe has pulled out of Dallas, Texas, by selling its trackage to Kansas City Southern and Dallas Area Rapid Transit, but on Dec. 14, 1993, the Warbonnet image was very much in evidence at the foot of Reunion Tower in the form of Dash 8 No. 945. **Mark R. Lynn**

Below: The 939 leads a coil steel train westward through the snow-covered mountains of northern Arizona near Chandler on Feb. 9, 1994. **James A. Speaker**

Model Dash 9-44CW
Builder: General Electric

Santa Fe continued to experience traffic increases in late 1993, with the trend projected to continue through 1995. With that in mind, the railroad again turned to General Electric for the latest motive power with an order for 50 Dash 9-44CWs. The Dash 9 series features the many advances in locomotive technology that evolved during production of the Dash 8s, including an alternating current traction option that should be available in late 1994.

Santa Fe's Dash 9s, numbered 600-649, were delivered from February to April 1994. The Dash 9 series features a new type of truck that is particularly striking on Santa Fe units because the silver paint accents the new design. The HiAd trucks are bolsterless and have traction motors that all face in the same direction, which maximizes adhesion and offers lower weight transfer than conventional trucks. All of these factors work to deliver more power to the rail in the form of increased tractive effort.

Facing page: A new Dash 9-44CW guides the SCHLA downgrade in Cajon Pass on March 13, 1994. **David Miller**

Top left: This view of the 601 at San Bernardino shows the bolsterless HiAd trucks, a new feature on the Dash 9s. **David Miller**

Left: Another view of the 609 at Summit, Calif., in Cajon Pass allows comparison to the trailing duo of Dash 8s. **David Miller**

◆ ◇ ◆ The Future

Will Santa Fe return to General Electric for a.c. technology when it becomes available, or will it look to EMD for locomotives equipped with a.c. power? Only time will tell, but EMD SD70MACs are running on the Santa Fe with coal trains off the Burlington Northern and their performance is very impressive.

Alternating current technology is based on the use of a.c. traction motors rather than the traditional direct current motors. The a.c. motors have no moving parts to wear out, and are not susceptible to flashovers and burnouts the way d.c. motors under heavy load are. Rectifiers are used to convert the d.c. power produced by the generator to a.c. Alternating current locomotives have a higher initial cost, but this should be recouped quickly by reduced motor maintenance.

Based on Santa Fe's aggressive motive power upgrade program over the last few years, the likelihood of a.c. technology being included in future locomotive orders is high. Most likely, the railroad will wait until GE's a.c. power has seen enough field testing to work out any problems, and then bids will be solicited from both major builders.

A harbinger of things to come, a Santa Fe Warbonnet pilots Burlington Northern's executive train at Moabi, Calif., on Feb. 1, 1994, as it returns from Super Bowl festivities in Pasadena. On June 30, 1994, Santa Fe and Burlington Northern announced their merger, making daily scenes of Warbonnets mixed with BN locomotives a liklihood once the Interstate Commerce Commission approves the alliance.
Mark R. Wayman

◆ ◇ ◆ Epilogue

On June 30, 1994, the Atchison, Topeka & Santa Fe Railway and the Burlington Northern Railroad announced that they had agreed to merge, confirming months of rumors and speculation by industry analysts. At first glance, because BN is nearly three times the size of the Santa Fe (22,316 miles versus 8,536 miles) it appears that BN will be the dominant partner in the merger. BN President and CEO Gerald Grinstein will be chairman of the new Burlington Northern & Santa Fe, while Santa Fe President and CEO Robert Krebs will assume the same roles for BNSF. Grinstein is approaching retirement age, and many feel that when the merger is consummated, he will step down and Krebs will assume the reins of the new company.

The Interstate Commerce Commission has agreed to take no longer than 14 months to render a decision after the filing of the formal merger application. The filing is expected to take place in October 1994, so a decision should be reached by the end of 1995. Mr. Krebs has stated that while the merger proceedings are taking place, the primary goal of the Santa Fe is to stay focused on the daily operation and improvement of the railroad.

To that end Santa Fe announced during the first week of August 1994 that 50 more Dash 9-44CWs would begin arriving in September 1994, and that 25 London-built EMD SD70Ms would arrive in the first quarter of 1995. The SD70M will be a new model for Santa Fe, and it should look great in the Warbonnet paint. These new units should address Santa Fe's locomotive shortage, but work on the physical plant is also being done to deal with bottlenecks caused by the booming business. For instance, Santa Fe is continuing its double-tracking project on the transcontinental main line to increase capacity. Some portions of the route are at saturation levels, with strong growth in Los Angeles-Chicago corridor traffic projected to continue.

There are many questions about the Burlington Northern & Santa Fe Railroad that will be answered by the passage of time. As this is being written, the biggest question among rail enthusiasts is what will the paint scheme of the merged company be? Will Burlington Northern Cascade green survive and end—once and for all—the Warbonnet era? Or will the Warbonnet scheme prevail as Mr. Krebs has said he would like to see (though could not guarantee)? The Warbonnet is arguably the most recognized and revered paint scheme in the history of railroading. As noted earlier in this book, the revival of the Warbonnet paint has been hailed as one of the most brilliant marketing and public relations moves ever made by a railroad. Hopefully, the Warbonnet will have the opportunity to continue to serve the new company. If, however, the era of the Warbonnet is truly over after the merger, we should consider ourselves fortunate to have witnessed a paint scheme that transcended simply being the colors worn by a locomotive. The Warbonnet symbolized the ties that the Santa Fe has with the great American Southwest. Those ties, Warbonnets or not, will live forever.

All-time Warbonnet Locomotive Summary

Current as of August 1994

MODEL	NUMBER	DATE	NOTES	TOTAL
BOXCAB	IL	1938	Rebuilt from IA, rebuilt to 83A (1953)	I
BOXCAB	I0L	1938	Rebuilt from IB; renumbered to IA (1941), 2611 (1948); rebuilt to 84A (1953)	I
			CLASS TOTAL	2
EIA/B	2A	1937	Renumbered 2L; rebuilt to 8IL (1952)	I
	2B	1937	B-unit; renumbered 2A; rebuilt to 80L (1952)	I
	3L	1938	Rebuilt to 82L (1953)	I
	3A	1938	Rebuilt to 82A (1953)	I
	4L	1938	Rebuilt to 80A (1953)	I
	4A	1938	Rebuilt to 8IA (1952)	I
	5L	1938	Rebuilt to 83L (1953)	I
	6L	1938	Rebuilt to 84L (1953)	I
	7L	1938	Rebuilt to 85L (1953)	I
	8L	1938	Rebuilt to 86L (1953)	I
	9L	1938	Rebuilt to 87L (1953)	I
			CLASS TOTAL	II
E3A/B	IIL, A	1939		2
			CLASS TOTAL	2
E6A/B	I2L, A	1940		2
	I3A	1941		
	I4L	1940		
	I5L, A	1941		2
			CLASS TOTAL	6
F3A/B	I6LABC-36LABC	1946-1948	32A wrecked 1949, rebuilt to 48A 1952	84
	32A (2nd)	1949	bought to replace 32A (Ist)	I
			CLASS TOTAL	85
F7A/B	37LABC-4ILABC	1949		20
	42LABC-47LABC	1952		24
	48A	1952	Rebuilt from 32A (Ist)	I
			CLASS TOTAL	45
DL-I09/DL-II0	50L/A	1940		2
			CLASS TOTAL	2

MODEL	NUMBER	DATE	NOTES	TOTAL
PAI-/PB-I	51LAB-52LAB	1946	51B-62B renumbered 63L-78L (1949)	6
	53LAB-58LAB	1947		18
	59LAB-62LAB	1948		12
	70LA-73LA	1948		8
			CLASS TOTAL	44
E8m	80L	1952	Rebuilt from 2L	1
	80A	1953	Rebuilt from 4L	1
	81L	1953	Rebuilt from 2A	1
	81A	1952	Rebuilt from 4A	1
	82L	1953	Rebuilt from 3L	1
	82A	1953	Rebuilt from 3A	1
	83L	1953	Rebuilt from 5L	1
	83A	1953	Rebuilt from IL	1
	84L	1953	Rebuilt from 6L	
	84A	1953	Rebuilt from 2611	1
	85L	1953	Rebuilt from 7L	1
	86L	1953	Rebuilt from 8L	1
	87L	1953	Rebuilt from 9L	1
			CLASS TOTAL	13
Fairbanks-Morse ERIE-BUILT	90ABC	1947		3
			CLASS TOTAL	3
FTA/B	158LABC-168LABC	1944-45	NOTE (I)	44
			CLASS TOTAL	44
F3A/B	200LABC-20ILABC	1948		8
			CLASS TOTAL	8
F7A/B	300LAB-305LAB	1949		18
	306LAB-312LAB	1950	Renumbered 325LAB-331LAB	21
	306LAB(2nd)-309LAB(2nd)	1952		12
	310LAB(2nd)-314LAB(2nd)	1953		15
	313LAB-316LAB	1951	Renumbered 332LAB-335LAB	12
	336LAB-340LAB	1953		15
	341LA-344LA	1953		8
			CLASS TOTAL	101

THE SECOND GENERATION

MODEL	NUMBER	DATE	NOTES	TOTAL
FP45	100-108	1967	Renumbered 5940-5948, see NOTE (2)	9
			CLASS TOTAL	9
U28CG	350-359	1966	Renumbered 7900-7909	10
			CLASS TOTAL	10

MODEL	NUMBER	DATE	NOTES	TOTAL
U30CG	400-405	1967	Renumbered 8000-8005	6
				CLASS TOTAL 6
GP60M	100-162	1990	NOTE (3)	63
				CLASS TOTAL 63
GP60B	325-347	1991		23
				CLASS TOTAL 23
Dash 8-40BW	500-559	1990		60
	560-582	1992		23
				CLASS TOTAL 83
Dash 8-40CW	800-866	1992		67
	867-926	1993	NOTE (4)	60
				CLASS TOTAL 127
Dash 8-41CW	927-951	1993	NOTE (5)	25
				CLASS TOTAL 25
Dash 9-44CW	600-649	1994		50
	650-699	1994		50
				CLASS TOTAL 100

NOTES

1) 167LABC delivered in freight paint, passenger gearing 1945. In 1946, 158LABC-166LABC and 168LABC were converted to passenger gearing.
All sets were painted in Warbonnet scheme at this time.

2) FP45 renumberings:

ORIG. NO.	2ND	3RD	4TH	5TH	CURRENT NO.
100	5940	5990	100	5990	90
101	5941	5991	104	5991	91
102	5942	5992	101	—	92
103	5943	5993	106	5993	93
104	5944	(wrecked and scrapped)			
105	5945	5995	107	5995	95
106	5946	5996	103	—	96
107	5947	5997	105	5997	97
108	5948	5998	102	5998	98

3) Nos.148, 152 wrecked at Corona, Calif., November 1990, scrapped January 1991.
4) No. 925 equipped with split cooling and electronic fuel injection.
5) Similar to Dash 8-40CW but all equipped with split cooling and delivered rated at 4,135 h.p.

REFERENCES

SANTA FE'S DIESEL FLEET, Joe McMillan
SANTA FE'S EARLY DIESEL DAZE, John B. McCall
SANTA FE 1992 ANNUAL, Kevin EuDaly